Quick Crockery Cooking

A One Foot in the Kitchen Cookbook

Written and Compiled by
CYNDI DUNCAN AND GEORGIE PATRICK

Illustrated by
COLETTE McLAUGHLIN

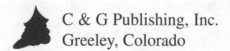

C & G Publishing, Inc.
Greeley, Colorado

Quick Crockery Cooking

Copyright © 1997
by Cyndi Duncan and Georgie Patrick

Library of Congress Catalog Card Number: 96-92795
ISBN 0-9626335-5-0
Printed in the United States of America

Illustrations and photograph by Colette McLaughlin
Graphic Design by Gregory Effinger, for
Colorado Independent Graphics, Advertising and Reproduction

Nutrition analysis has been calculated on Mastercook II software.

To the best of our knowledge, all information included in this book is correct and complete. The publisher and authors offer no guarantees and disclaim any liability attributed to its use.

Published by C & G Publishing, Inc.
P.O. Box 5199
Greeley, Colorado
For orders and information: (800) 925-3172

To the Georgies and the Cyndis of the world

who pray for snow days

who think teenagers are people

who cry at parades and sporting events

who have more holiday decorations than clothes

who store 30 years of family photos in 30 year-old shoe boxes

and who are overworked and underpaid,

this book's for you!

Contents

Introduction

Our most requested title to date, *Quick Crockery Cooking*, was born from the cry of working women who literally only have time for one foot in the kitchen. The book started out as a quick meal book but soon evolved into a series, *One Foot in the Kitchen*.

Early on it became apparent that Cyndi and I had completely different ideas about what was quick and how best to get the end result. Cyndi is one of those incredibly organized cooks who does those wonderfully domesticated things in the kitchen. You know the type. The one who grows her own fruits and vegetables, always has cookies in the cookie jar, and can feed an army of teenagers in fifteen minutes. Did I mention that she makes spaghetti sauce from scratch? So, it isn't any wonder that her view of quick cooking leans a little towards the make-ahead approach. (You know, I think I'm the one who introduced her to canned cream of mushroom soup.) Cyndi's freezer is filled with wonderful sauces, kraut burgers, soups and Mexican food that enables her to fix a gourmet delight in a matter of minutes.

I, on the other hand, don't feel anything is quick if at some point in time I had to spend hours preparing it. My kitchen is a catchall for the thousands of pieces of paper that seem to come through my hands daily, and usually I have to make room on the counter to cook. Don't get me wrong, I like to cook for special occasions and can usually make a pretty good showing for myself. It's the day-to-day cooking where I fall apart, and I really feel that there are more Georgies than Cyndis in this world. I'm on a first name basis with the people behind the counter at the deli, my pork chops are stuffed at the meat counter and my spaghetti sauce comes in a jar. You know what? I don't even feel guilty. Actually, sometimes I even feel a little smug.

The slow cooker was especially invented for us Georgies. It allows us to take the little time we have for cooking and make the best of it. But, I have to admit sometimes I look at the Cyndis in this world and wonder if they have an extra package in their freezer for me.

Georgie

Footnotes from Cyndi and Georgie

These "footnotes" are not necessarily gospel, but some that we have found useful in planning our meals and cooking with our slow cookers. We have geared these recipes to be QUICK and easy to prepare; grocery stores offer so many conveniences that cooking doesn't have to be a difficult project. We have chosen and created recipes with ingredients that most of us keep in our cupboards or that are easily obtained from the store. Slow cooking has returned with Quick Crockery Cooking.

Seasonings, spices, onions and garlic grow in flavor when cooked in a slow cooker.

Buy foods frozen, canned and already chopped to save time.

Buy meat already boned and cut into pieces. It is still important to rinse meat to remove fat and bone particles. This is a step in cooking that should become habit. Browning meat before placing in slow cooker is strictly personal preference.

Presoaking beans shortens cooking time. Drain the soaking water and replace with enough fresh water to cover beans by about an inch before cooking.

Milk, sour cream and other dairy products are added later in the cooking cycle because they often separate or curdle with cooking for long periods.

Very little water is needed in slow cooking recipes, since most of the natural juices are retained.

Start frozen foods in cold slow cooker and add about 2 hours to cooking time.

"Bake" cakes and breads by pouring batter into a coffee can and placing it inside slow cooker; read instruction booklet.

If slow cooking at an altitude above 3500 feet, add 1 to 2 hours to cooking time.

Slow cooking saves energy, costing only 2 to 3 cents for 10 hours cooking time.

All recipes are designated to cook on low; cook on high to cut time in half.

Notes:

Appetizers

Beverages

HOLIDAY WASSAIL

1 18-ounce can pineapple juice
8 cups apple juice or cider
3 tablespoons lemon juice
2 tablespoons sugar
1/4 teaspoon nutmeg
6 whole cloves
1 cinnamon stick

Combine all ingredients in slow cooker. Cover and heat on low 2 to 3 hours or until ready to serve. Ladle into cups and garnish by putting cinnamon stick in each cup. Serves 12.

Per serving: 123 calories; 0.9 fat grams

 Your home will smell so-o-o good.

WARM ORANGE WASSAIL

2 12-ounce cans frozen orange juice concentrate
2/3 cup sugar
6 cinnamon sticks
8 teaspoons whole cloves
1 1/2 cups vodka

Mix orange juice according to directions on can right in slow cooker. Add sugar and spices. Cover and cook on low 2 to 3 hours. Just before serving add vodka and let warm about 15 minutes. Pour into warm punch bowl, straining out the spices. Keep warm on a warming tray. Garnish by floating orange slices. Serves 10.

Per serving: 253 Calories, 0.6 fat grams

SPICED TEA TO WARM THE SOUL

1 teaspoon nutmeg
1 teaspoon cinnamon
1 teaspoon allspice
1/4 cup black tea
2 quarts warm water
1 cup sugar
1 cup orange juice
1/2 cup lemon juice
1 quart cranberry juice

Combine nutmeg, cinnamon, allspice and tea in a large tea ball or wrap in a piece of cheese cloth. Place in slow cooker. Add water. Cover and heat on high 1 hour. Add sugar, orange juice, lemon juice and cranberry juice. Stir. Cover and heat to serving temperature. Remove tea ball and pour juice mixture into warm punch bowl. Serve in cups garnished with a lemon slice. Serves 12.

Per serving: 128 calories; 0.2 fat grams

HOT BUTTERED RUM

2 quarts water
1 pound butter
1 pound brown sugar
1 pound powdered sugar
1 1/2 teaspoons cinnamon
1 1/2 teaspoons nutmeg
Rum
Vanilla ice cream
Cinnamon sticks

Combine water, butter, sugars, cinnamon and nutmeg in slow cooker. Cover and heat on high 1 hour. Reduce heat to low. Heat until ready to serve. Have warm mugs ready. Measure 1 jigger of rum into mug, then ladle sugar mixture into cup. Top off with dollop of ice cream or whipped cream and a sprinkle of sugar. Offer a cinnamon stick for stirring drink. Serves 8.

Per serving: 434 calories; 19.5 fat grams

HOT SANGRIA

4 cups water
1 cup sugar
Peel of 1/2 lemon
Juice from that lemon
18 whole cloves
1 10-ounce package frozen mixed fruit in
    syrup, thawed
4/5 quart dry, red wine
1 cup brandy

Combine water, sugar, lemon peel, lemon juice, cloves and mixed fruit in slow cooker. Cover and heat on low 2 to 3 hours. About 30 minutes before serving, add wine and brandy. Cover and heat to serving temperature. Serve in hot pottery mugs, each garnished with lemon slice, plus a cinnamon stick for stirring. Makes about 20 servings.

Per serving: 126 calories; 1.2 fat grams

OLD ENGLISH WASSAIL

8 cups apple juice or cider
2 cups cranberry juice
3/4 cup sugar
2 cinnamon sticks
1 teaspoon whole allspice
1 small orange studded with whole cloves
1 cup rum, optional

Put all ingredients in slow cooker. Cover and cook on low 4 to 8 hours. Serve right from slow cooker. Serves 12.

Per serving: 179 calories; 1.6 fat grams

 What a great way to welcome guests! It smells wonderful and tastes even better.

STARTER MEATBALLS

2 pounds lean ground beef
1 cup seasoned Italian bread crumbs
1 package onion soup mix
3 eggs
1 can cranberry sauce
1 cup light brown sugar, not packed
1 12-ounce bottle chili sauce
1 chili bottle of water
1 cup sauerkraut, drained

In large mixing bowl, combine ground beef, bread crumbs, soup mix and eggs. Form into balls. Brown in skillet and drain. Remove to slow cooker. In another mixing bowl, combine remaining ingredients and pour over meatballs. Cover and cook on low 3 to 4 hours; QUICK time on high 2 hours. Serves 15.

Per serving: 281 calories; 13.8 fat grams

BEEF DIP

1 pound lean ground beef
1/2 onion, chopped
1 clove garlic, minced
1 cup tomato sauce
1/4 cup catsup
3/4 teaspoon oregano
1 teaspoon sugar
1 8-ounce package cream cheese
1/3 cup parmesan cheese, grated

Brown ground beef and drain. Pour into slow cooker. Add onion, garlic, tomato sauce, catsup, oregano and sugar. Cover and cook on low 3 to 4 hours. About 30 minutes before serving, turn slow cooker to high. Add cream cheese and parmesan cheese. Stir to melt. Reduce heat. Cover and cook on low until ready to serve, stirring occasionally. Serve with corn chips or crackers. Serves 10.

Per serving: 229 calories; 18.2 fat grams

QUICK CHILE CON QUESO

1 pound processed American cheese
1 10-ounce can tomatoes and green chiles

Cube cheese into slow cooker. Pour tomatoes and green chilies over cheese. Cover and cook on low 1 to 2 hours, stirring occasionally. If you prefer this dip a little spicier, add some chopped jalapenos. Add a little water if it gets too thick as it cooks. Ladle into dish to serve or leave it right in slow cooker and let guests serve themselves. Serves 15.

Per serving: 116 calories; 9.5 fat grams

 To save time, buy tomatoes and green chiles already chopped.

Make this one a little different, but just as QUICK, by adding 1 16-ounce can hot chili with beans.

BARBECUED HOT DOGS FOR A CROWD

4 packages wieners or large package of
    cocktail wieners
1 tablespoon butter, melted
1/2 cup onions, chopped
2 teaspoons mustard
8 teaspoons Worcestershire sauce
2 tablespoons sugar
1/2 cup tomato catsup
2 teaspoons vinegar

Cut wieners in bite-size pieces. Put in slow cooker. Combine all other ingredients and pour over wieners. Cover and cook on low 3 to 4 hours. QUICK time on high 1 hour. When ready to serve, remove from slow cooker to a serving dish, or leave in slow cooker to have guest serve themselves to this all-time favorite snack. Serves 20.

Per serving: 55 calories; 3.9 fat grams

CHILE CON QUESO

1 small onion, minced
1 clove garlic, minced
1/4 teaspoon ground cumin
1 14-ounce can tomatoes, chopped
2 4-ounce cans green chiles, chopped
1/2 pound processed American cheese
1 8-ounce package cream cheese
1 cup sour cream
Salt and pepper to taste

Spray slow cooker with nonstick spray. Place all ingredients into slow cooker. Cover and cook 3 to 4 hours, stirring occasionally. Serve with nacho chips. Serves 15.

Per serving: 154 calories; 13.3 fat grams

HOT CRAB "FONDUE"

1 5-ounce jar processed American cheese spread
1 8-ounce package cream cheese
1 7 1/2-ounce can Alaskan King Crab, drained
1/4 cup light cream
1/2 teaspoon Worcestershire sauce
1/4 teaspoon garlic salt
1/2 teaspoon cayenne pepper

Combine all ingredients in slow cooker. Cover and cook on low 2 to 3 hours, stirring occasionally. Add more cream if mixture becomes too thick while warming. Serves 10.

Per serving: 162 calories; 13.6 fat grams

Notes:

Soups

BEEF STEW

6 carrots, sliced
6 potatoes, sliced into bite-sized pieces
1 1/2 pounds round steak or stew meat, cut
    into 1-inch cubes
4 cups of water plus 4 tablespoons bouillon
    granules or 4 bouillon cubes
1 teaspoon Worcestershire sauce
1 teaspoon garlic salt
2 bay leaves
1 1/2 teaspoons salt
1/2 teaspoon pepper
1/2 teaspoon celery salt
1 stalk celery and tops, sliced
1 15-ounce can green beans
1 15-ounce can tomato sauce

Prepare and put all ingredients in slow cooker in order given. Cover and cook on low 10 to 12 hours. Serves 8.

Per serving: 260 calories; 10.6 fat grams

 Hot biscuits are excellent with stew.

VEGETABLE STEW

2 large onions, sliced
1 stalk celery, sliced
3 cloves garlic, minced, or 1 1/2 teaspoons
    garlic powder
2 large tomatoes, chopped
4 medium zucchini, sliced
2 medium green peppers, sliced
1/4 cup parsley, chopped
3 tablespoons vinegar
2 teaspoons thyme
1 teaspoon salt
1 teaspoon sugar
1/2 teaspoon pepper

Combine all ingredients in slow cooker. Cover and cook on low 8 to 10 hours. Serve with fruit and bread. Serves 4.

Per serving: 74 calories; 0.7 fat grams

 Georgie prefers corn bread with any stew.

CURRIED CHICKEN STEW

2 chicken breasts, cooked and diced
1/4 cup onion, chopped finely
1 tart apple, chopped, not peeled
1/4 cup carrot, chopped
2 tablespoons green pepper, chopped
3 tablespoons flour
1/2 teaspoon curry powder
4 cups chicken broth
1 16-ounce can tomatoes, chopped
1 tablespoon parsley
1 teaspoon sugar
1/4 teaspoon salt
2 whole cloves
1/4 teaspoon pepper
2 teaspoons lemon juice.

Mix chicken, onion, apple, carrot, green pepper, flour and curry powder together in slow cooker. Add remaining ingredients and stir. Cover and cook on low 4 to 6 hours. Ladle into soup bowls with a side of rice. Serves 6.

Per serving: 194 calories; 3.5 fat grams

 Foot Note For a variety, add thin noodles, broken spaghetti, macaroni, rice or barley.

BASIC CHILI

Cyndi's family likes homemade cinnamon rolls or corn bread with chili. Traditionally, chili is served on the first snow day of the season.

2 pounds lean ground beef
1 medium onion, chopped
4 garlic cloves, chopped
3 to 4 tablespoons chili powder
2 14-ounce cans tomatoes, chopped
1 30-ounce can beans in chili sauce
1 8-ounce can tomato sauce
1 teaspoon salt
1/2 teaspoon pepper
1/2 teaspoon ground cumin
1/2 teaspoon oregano, optional

Brown ground beef in a skillet; drain. Add onion, garlic and chili powder. Cook for another 5 minutes. Pour into slow cooker. Add remaining ingredients and stir. Cover and cook on low 8 to 10 hours. Serves 8.

Per serving: 456 calories; 25.9 fat grams

 Vary this recipe by using kidney beans in place of the chili beans and by adding chopped green pepper and celery.

BOB'S CHILI

1 pound lean ground beef
1 teaspoon sage
1 30-ounce can beans in chili sauce
2 tablespoons chili powder
1 teaspoon sugar or honey
1 cup celery, chopped
1 14-ounce can tomatoes
1 cup tomato juice
2 large onions, chopped
1 teaspoon salt
1/2 teaspoon pepper

Brown ground beef and drain. Pour into slow cooker and add remaining ingredients. Stir and cover. Cook on low 8 to 10 hours. Serves 8.

Per serving: 295 calories; 13.9 fat grams

Once when Georgie was away from home for several days, her husband, Bob cooked chili three or four times that week. According to the Patrick children, none of the recipes he used were successful. They were more than relieved when Georgie returned home. When asked what they would like for dinner, the response was an overwhelming, "No Chili!." In spite of the cold reception to his cooking, Bob continues to make chili. This is one of his favorites.

CHILI

2 pounds lean ground beef or turkey
1 large onion, finely chopped
1 green pepper, chopped, optional
2 cloves garlic, minced
3 tablespoons chili powder
1 teaspoon salt
1 teaspoon pepper
1 teaspoon cumin, optional
1/2 teaspoon oregano
1 30-ounce can chili beans in chili gravy
1 15-ounce can red kidney beans, optional
2 15-ounce cans tomatoes already chopped
    or crushed
1 8-ounce can tomato sauce

Brown beef or turkey and drain. Pour into slow cooker. Put all other ingredients in slow cooker. Cover and cook on low 10 to 12 hours. Serves 8 to 10.

Per serving: 639 calories; 26.6 fat grams

Foot Notes

The QUICKest way I have found to chop vegetables is to put them all in a blender with one of the cans of tomatoes and blend them. This is good, too, if someone in the family does not like onions or chunks of tomatoes, when blended, they are not easily detected.

Substituting turkey will make this lower in calories and fat.

TURKEY CHILI

2 pounds ground turkey
2 cloves garlic, minced
1 medium onion, chopped
1 medium green pepper, chopped
1 medium yellow or red pepper, cut up
1 16-ounce can tomatoes, cut up
1 10-ounce can green chiles and tomatoes,
   already chopped
1 15-ounce can tomato sauce
1 cup water
1 8-ounce can garbanzo beans, drained
1 15-ounce can kidney beans, drained
2 tablespoons chili powder
1 teaspoon dry mustard
1 tablespoon sugar
1/2 teaspoon salt
1/4 teaspoon white pepper

Brown turkey on high in slow cooker. Add garlic, onion, and both peppers. Simmer 5 minutes. Drain any fat. Add remaining ingredients. Cover and cook on low 8 to 10 hours. Serve with hot corn bread. Serves 8.

Per Serving: 507 calories; 12.2 fat grams

SOUTHERN VEGETABLE SOUP

1 ham hock
2 quarts water (8 cups)
2 14-ounce cans tomatoes, coarsely chopped
3 medium potatoes, peeled and sliced
1 8-ounce can corn
1 large onion, chopped
1 can butter beans
1 cup okra, sliced
Salt and pepper to taste

Combine all ingredients in slow cooker. Stir. Cover and cook on low 8 to 10 hours. This soup is really good with cornbread. Serves 8.

Per serving: 178 calories; 3.0 fat grams

CABBAGE SOUP

1 pound lean ground beef
4 potatoes, peeled and diced
4 carrots, peeled and diced
4 cups cabbage, shredded
1/4 cup onion, chopped
1 10-ounce can tomato soup
Salt and pepper to taste
4 cups water

Brown ground beef in skillet; drain and pour into slow cooker. Place remaining ingredients in slow cooker, making sure that water covers vegetables. Cover and cook on low 6 to 8 hours. Serves 10 to 12.

Per serving: 183 calories; 9.9 fat grams

 If you prefer a juicier soup, add more water.

This hearty soup is great on a cold evening.

VEGETABLE BEEF SOUP

2 cups leftover roast beef, steak or ground
    beef, or a meaty soup bone
1 15-ounce can tomatoes, already cut up
1 large onion, chopped
3 or 4 carrots, sliced
4 stalks celery, sliced
3 large potatoes, diced
4 cups water
1 teaspoon salt
1 teaspoon coarsely ground pepper
4 beef bouillon cubes (broth saved from
    cooking a roast adds extra flavor)
1 16-ounce package frozen vegetables
1 cup cabbage, shredded

Put all ingredients in slow cooker. Cover and cook on low 10 to 12 hours. Serves 8.

Per serving: 218 calories; 9.9 fat grams

This is a good soup to prepare the night before you plan to serve it and let it cook on low all night.

To vary this recipe, add 1/2 cup barley, noodles or rice 1 hour before serving. Cover and cook on high until ready to

BEEF AND PINTO BEAN SOUP

This is a longtime favorite of L. G., Cyndi's husband, and his family.

1 1-pound package dried pinto beans
1 large meaty beef or ham bone
1 medium onion, chopped
1 cup celery, chopped
1 teaspoon salt
1 teaspoon coarsely ground pepper

Soak beans overnight. Rinse and place in slow cooker. Add other ingredients. Cover and cook on low 10 to 12 hours. When ready to serve, pick meat off the bones and stir into the beans. Serve over corn bread with coleslaw on the side. Serves 6.

Per serving: 308 calories; 3.9 fat grams

MINESTRONE

4 cups beef broth
2 cups water
2 cups leftover roast beef, cut up or shredded, or a meaty beef bone
1 tablespoon basil, crushed
1 teaspoon garlic salt
1 teaspoon oregano
1/2 teaspoon thyme
1 medium onion, diced
3 carrots, diced
1 cup celery with tops, sliced
1 10-ounce package frozen vegetables
1 15-ounce can garbanzo beans
1 cup small elbow macaroni
2 teaspoons salt
1 zucchini, sliced
1 cup cabbage, shredded
1 15-ounce can tomatoes

Put all ingredients in slow cooker. Cover and cook on low 8 to 10 hours. Serve with parmesan cheese and a large loaf of warm sour dough bread. Serves 12.

Per serving: 291 calories; 8.6 fat grams

Broth left from roasts adds extra flavor to your soups.

GREEN CHILE CHEESE SOUP

1 1/2 cups chicken or turkey, shredded or cubed
1 medium onion, chopped
1 cup celery, sliced
3 potatoes, peeled, diced
3 cups chicken broth or bouillon
1 16-ounce cream-style corn
1 8-ounce can green chiles, chopped
1 2-ounce jar pimientos, chopped
1 pound light processed American cheese
Chives

Put all ingredients except cheese in slow cooker. Stir just to mix. Cover and cook on low 8 hours. One hour before serving, turn slow cooker to high. Add cheese, cover and stir occasionally until cheese is melted. Lower heat until ready to serve. Ladle into soup bowls and top with chives and shredded Monterey Jack cheese with flour tortillas on the side. Serves 6 to 8.

Per serving: 380 calories; 21.4 fat grams

This is a great use of leftover chicken or turkey.

Everyone will love this soup! If you like it a bit spicier, use the hot processed American cheese.

GREEN CHILE STEW

3 pounds lean, boned round steak or roast,
    cut in bite-sized pieces
1 10-ounce can green chiles, diced
4 onions, chopped
4 fresh tomatoes, peeled and chopped, or 1
    15-ounce can tomatoes
1 cup water
1 1/2 teaspoons salt
3 cloves garlic, chopped, or 3/4 teaspoon
    garlic powder
1 teaspoon cumin
1/2 teaspoon oregano

Place all ingredients in slow cooker. Cover and cook on low 8 to 10 hours. Serves 6

Per serving: 485 calories; 27.8 fat grams

 This soup is great standing alone, served with a salad and tortillas; but try it as a salsa for smothered burritos.

CHEESE TOPPED ONION SOUP

4 large onions, sliced
1 teaspoon coarsely ground pepper
3 14-ounce cans beef broth
1 broth can water
1 envelope onion soup mix
Sliced French bread
Olive oil
Cut garlic clove
Muenster cheese, shredded

Put onions, pepper, beef broth, water and soup mix in slow cooker. Cover and cook on low 8 to 10 hours. About 30 minutes before serving, preheat oven to 475°. Brush bread lightly with olive oil. Rub both sides of bread with garlic clove. Sprinkle one side with cheese. Ladle soup from slow cooker into ovenproof bowls. Put a slice of bread, cheese side up, on top of each serving. Bake at 475° until cheese is golden brown (about 5 minutes). Serves 6.

Per serving: 224 calories; 8.4 fat grams

ONION SOUP

5 medium onions, sliced
2 tablespoons butter
White pepper to taste
1 bay leaf
1/4 cup dry sherry
3 cans beef consomme
3 cans chicken broth
French bread
Parmesan
3 cups Swiss cheese, grated

In skillet, saute onions in butter until light brown. Pour into slow cooker. Add pepper, bay leaf, sherry, consomme and chicken broth. Cover and cook on low 8 to 10 hours. While soup is cooking, lay out 6 thickly sliced pieces of French bread to dry a little. About 15 minutes before serving, preheat oven to 375°. Ladle soup into 6 ovenproof soup bowls. Place a piece of bread on each bowl of soup and sprinkle generously with Swiss cheese and parmesan cheese. Bake at 375° 10 minutes or until cheese is slightly brown. Serves 6.

Per serving: 412 calories; 22.5 fat grams

POTATO SOUP

8 potatoes, peeled and diced
2 carrots, finely shredded
2 stalks celery, sliced
2 onions, chopped
5 chicken bouillon cubes
5 cups water
1 1/2 teaspoons salt
1/2 teaspoon pepper
1 12-ounce can evaporated milk
Chives
Parsley

Prepare vegetables and place in slow cooker. Add bouillon cubes, water, salt and pepper. Cover and cook on low 6 to 8 hours. About 2 hours before serving, if possible, add milk and mash potatoes with masher. If not possible, add milk at the start of cooking and add some instant potatoes to thicken. Ladle into soup bowls and garnish with just a bit of chives and parsley. Serves 8.

Per serving: 147 calories; 3.5 fat grams

GREEN CHILI

3 1/2 - 4 pounds lean pork, diced
24 to 30 green chiles, cut into strips (can be
    fresh or 30-ounce can)
1 teaspoon salt
1 teaspoon pepper
1 tablespoon garlic powder
Dash of cumin
1 28-ounce can tomatoes
1 16-ounce can tomatoes, chopped
2 medium onions, chopped
1 cup water
Cheddar cheese, optional

Brown pork and put in slow cooker with all the juices. Add remaining ingredients. Cook on low 6 to 8 hours. Garnish with cheese. Serves 12.

Per serving: 283 calories; 17.0 fat grams

 Serve as a side dish with any Mexican food, or use to smother burritos.

CALDO CON QUESO

2 1/2 cups water
1 medium tomato, peeled and chopped
1 7-ounce can green chiles, cut in strips
1/4 teaspoon pepper
1 teaspoon garlic salt
1 13-ounce can evaporated milk
1 10-ounce can cream of potato soup
1 10-ounce can cream of onion soup
8 ounces Monterey Jack cheese, cut in
　　　small pieces (about 2 cups)

Combine all ingredients, except cheese, in slow cooker. Cover and cook on low 4 to 6 hours. At serving time, ladle soup over cheese into soup bowls. Serves 6 to 8.

Per serving: 204 calories; 13.3 fat grams

 Cyndi sometimes adds leftover chicken or turkey to this recipe to make a little heartier soup.

CHICKEN NOODLE SOUP

Chicken soup is good for the soul and colds (Cyndi's theory!)

2 quarts water (can use 8 cups canned
    chicken broth and 2 chicken bouillon
    cubes instead of water and 5 cubes)
5 chicken bouillon cubes
1 - 1 1/2 teaspoons salt
1/2 teaspoon pepper
1/2 teaspoon parsley
1/2 teaspoon oregano
2 bay leaves
1 medium onion, chopped
3 stalks of celery, sliced
1/2 cup carrots, sliced
3 or 4 chicken breasts, cut into bite sized
    pieces (or use shredded leftover chicken)
2 cups uncooked noodles

Combine all ingredients, except noodles, in slow cooker. Cover and cook on low 8 to 10 hours. About 45 minutes before serving, cook noodles according to directions on package. Drain and add to soup in slow cooker. Heat on high to desired serving temperature; lower heat and cook together about 15 minutes. Serve with generous hunks of your favorite bread. Serves 10.

Per serving: 118 calories; 1.4 fat grams

 To save time, cook noodles the night before. Rinse, cool and store in refrigerator until ready to add to soup stock.

CHICKEN CHILE SOUP

2 1/2 cups water
1 teaspoon lemon pepper seasoning
1 teaspoon cumin seeds
4 chicken breasts
1 garlic clove, minced
1 cup onion, chopped
2 9-ounce packages frozen white corn, thawed
2 4-ounce cans diced green chiles
1 teaspoon ground cumin
2 to 3 tablespoon lime juice
2 15-ounce cans Great Northern beans, undrained
2/3 cup tortilla chips, crushed
2/3 cup Monterey Jack cheese (reduced fat cheese, if desired)

Combine all ingredients, expect tortilla chips and cheese, in slow cooker. Stir. Cover and cook on low 8 to 10 hours. To serve, place 1 tablespoon each of tortilla chips and cheese in 8 soup bowls. Ladle hot soup over cheese. Serve with salsa and warm tortillas. If you have an extra few minutes, butter the tortillas and place on a cookie sheet. Bake in oven at 400° for five minutes. Cut into wedges. Serves 8.

Per serving: 690 calories; 11.3 fat grams

This soup is a nice change for Super Bowl Sunday!!

Kitchen shears are great for cutting tortillas. Use them to save time cutting meats, chiles, etc. They just happen to be Georgie's favorite cooking tool.

VEGETABLE TACO SOUP

1 pound chicken breasts, skinned and
    boned, cut in bite-size pieces, or use
    leftover chicken breast
    meat, cut up
2 15-ounce cans tomatoes, chopped
2 14-ounce cans chicken broth
1 4-ounce can green chiles, chopped
1 10-ounce can enchilada sauce
1 10-ounce package frozen vegetables
1/2 teaspoon chili powder
6 corn tortillas
1/4 cup fresh cilantro, chopped
3/4 cup reduced-fat Monterey Jack
    cheese, shredded
Green taco sauce

Combine chicken, tomatoes, broth, chiles, enchilada sauce, vegetables and chili powder. Cover and cook on low 6 to 8 hours. Fifteen minutes before serving, preheat oven to 425°. Cut tortillas into 1/2-inch strips and lay on a cookie sheet; spray with nonstick cooking spray. Bake in oven 5 minutes or until golden brown. Ladle soup into bowls. Top with tortilla strips, cilantro and cheese. Serve with green taco sauce. Serves 10.

Per serving: 208 calories; 8.1 grams

 If you don't have time to prepare tortillas, use packaged chips.

SOUTHWESTERN SOUP

2 chicken breasts, diced
2 quarts chicken broth (4 10-ounce cans
    broth, plus 2 cups water)
1 10-ounce can tomatoes and green
    chiles, chopped
1 14-ounce can corn with green and red peppers
1 14-ounce pinto beans, drained
1 tablespoon cilantro, chopped
1 medium onion, finely diced
3 garlic cloves, minced
1 teaspoon ground cumin
2 tablespoons chili powder
1 package taco seasoning mix

Combine all ingredients in slow cooker. Stir.
Cover and cook on low 8 to 10 hours. Ladle into
soup bowls with sides of guacamole, black olives,
tortilla and Monterey Jack cheese. Serves 10.

Per serving: 197 calories; 3.8 fat grams

 Georgie likes this soup with shredded
cheese and corn chips sprinkled on top.

CHICKEN BARLEY SOUP

1 1/2 cups cooked chicken, diced
1 16-ounce can tomatoes, cut up
1/2 cup carrots, sliced
1/2 cup celery, sliced
1 3-ounce can mushrooms, drained, sliced
3 teaspoons instant chicken bouillon granules
1 bay leaf
1/4 teaspoon ground thyme
5 cups water
1/2 cup barley
1/2 cup Monterey Jack cheese, shredded

Combine all ingredients in slow cooker. Cover and cook on low 8 to 10 hours. Serve in soup bowls with some garlic bread. Garnish with a little Monterey Jack cheese. Serves 6.

Per serving: 166 calories; 4.0 fat grams

 To save time, buy tomatoes and mushrooms already cut up.

BROCCOLI CHEESE SOUP

1 large head of broccoli, washed and
   chopped
2 cups water
4 chicken bouillon cubes
2 cups milk
1/4 to 1/2 cup flour
1/2 cup half & half or evaporated milk
2 cups processed American cheese, cubed

Place prepared broccoli in slow cooker. Add water and bouillon cubes. Cover and cook on low 3 to 4 hours. One hour before serving, turn slow cooker to high. Mix milk and flour together, and add to broccoli, stirring until thickened. Reduce heat to low. Add half and half and cheese. Stir occasionally until cheese is melted. Ladle into soup bowls. Serves 6.

Per serving: 248 calories; 17.1 fat grams

Use 1 10-ounce package frozen, chopped broccoli if you don't have fresh broccoli. It's a QUICK alternative.

Vary this soup by adding a little grated carrot and chopped onion with the broccoli.

CREAM OF CHICKEN POTATO SOUP

6 cups water
3 medium potatoes, diced
1 small onion, diced
1 stalk celery, sliced
1/4 teaspoon pepper
1/4 teaspoon garlic salt
2 packets instant cream of chicken soup mix
4 slices American cheese
6 cups milk

Combine water, potatoes, onion, celery, pepper, garlic salt and soup mix in slow cooker. Cover and cook on low 4 to 6 hours. Stir in cheese and milk. Heat to desired serving temperature (about one hour). Serves 10.

Per serving: 290 calories; 18.5 fat grams

 Reduce calories and fat by using low-fat milk in your recipes.

CLAM CHOWDER

2 7-ounce cans minced clams, drained
1/2 cup celery, finely diced
1 medium onion, finely diced
4 medium potatoes, diced
1 1/2 cups water
3 tablespoons white wine, optional
1/2 teaspoon salt
1/2 teaspoon white pepper
1/8 teaspoon thyme
3 tablespoons flour
1 1/2 cups milk
1 cup half and half
Parsley

Combine clams, celery, onion, potatoes, water, wine and seasonings in slow cooker. Cover and cook on low 4 to 6 hours. Turn slow cooker to high. Mix flour, milk, and half and half in mixing bowl; add to clam mixture in slow cooker. Stir occasionally until thickened. Do not let mixture boil. Ladle into soup bowls and garnish with parsley. Serves 4 to 6.

Per serving: 248 calories; 7.3 fat grams

GOOD OLD-FASHIONED CORN CHOWDER

1/4 pound lean salt pork, or bacon, diced finely
1 large onion, chopped
1 cup celery, diced
2 tablespoons butter or margarine
1 cup water
2 14-ounce cans cream-style corn
1/4 teaspoon pepper
2 cups milk
1 12-ounce can evaporated milk

Saute salt pork slowly until crisp and golden; drain on paper towels. Saute onion and celery in butter just until barely tender. Place pork, onion and celery in slow cooker. Stir in water, corn and pepper. Cover and cook on low 4 to 6 hours. Add both milks. Heat to desired serving temperature. Ladle into soup bowls. Serve with crackers or buttered toast. Serves 6.

Per serving: 395 calories; 25.5 fat grams

FAVORITE BEAN SOUP

2 cups mixed dried beans plus water for
    soaking overnight
2 quarts water
1/2 pound ham, chopped
1 teaspoon salt
1 large onion, chopped, or 1 tablespoon
    onion flakes
1 16-ounce can tomatoes, chopped
1 teaspoon chili powder
2 teaspoons lemon juice

Wash and cover beans with water; soak overnight. Next morning, rinse beans and transfer to slow cooker. Add remaining ingredients, cover and cook on low 8 to 10 hours. Serve in soup bowls with corn bread. Serves 10.

Per serving: 194 calories; 3.1 fat grams

 To perk up your corn bread, add green chiles and shredded cheddar cheese to your mix.

Soups
Page 44

NAVY BEAN SOUP

2 cups navy beans
3 quarts water
1 ham bone
1/2 cup instant mashed potatoes
3 onions, finely chopped
1 stalk celery, chopped
1 clove garlic, minced
1/4 cup parsley

Place all ingredients in slow cooker. Stir until potatoes are well mixed. Cover and cook on low 8 to 10 hours. Remove ham bone before serving. Serves 6 to 8.

Per serving: 233 calories; 3.1 fat grams

CREAM OF ZUCCHINI SOUP

6 medium zucchini, cut in chunks, not peeled
1 medium onion, chopped
1 large garlic clove, minced
1 teaspoon salt
1/2 teaspoon pepper
1 tablespoon flour
3 14-ounce cans chicken broth

Mix all ingredients together in slow cooker. Cover and cook on high 2 hours. Remove from slow cooker and cool about 15 minutes. Put in blender and puree. Return to slow cooker and warm to serving temperature. Serves 6.

Per serving: 89 calories; 2.3 fat grams

This soup can be prepared the night before and served chilled for lunch or dinner the next day. Garnish with a sprig of mint or parsley and croutons on the side.

LIGHT AND HEALTHY BEAN SOUP

1 16-ounce can seasoned tomatoes
1 14-ounce can chicken broth
1 cup salsa
2 cups water
1 8-ounce can corn
1 16-ounce can garbanzo beans, rinsed and drained
1 16-ounce can kidney beans, rinsed and drained
1 15-ounce can black beans, rinsed and drained
1 large onion, chopped
1 clove garlic, minced
1 medium green pepper, chopped
1/2 teaspoon ground thyme
1/2 teaspoon oregano leaves
1/4 teaspoon basil leaves, crushed slightly
1/4 cup cilantro, chopped
1/2 cup uncooked white rice

Put all ingredients into slow cooker. Stir. Cover and cook on low 6 to 8 hours. Serve with warmed tortillas or fresh, crusty bread. Serves 8 to 10.

Per serving: 551 calories; 5.4 fat grams

HEARTY COLD DAY SOUP

3 to 4 links Italian sausage
Nonstick cooking spray
2 teaspoons cooking oil
2 cups onion, chopped
1 10-ounce can beef bouillon or 2 bouillon
    cubes and 1 1/2 cups water
5 cups water
1/4 cup vinegar
1 15-ounce canned kidney beans
1 15-ounce can tomato juice
1/2 6-ounce can tomato paste
1 medium head cabbage, chopped
2 large potatoes, scrubbed and diced
1 teaspoon salt
1/2 teaspoon pepper
1/2 teaspoon garlic salt
1/2 teaspoon garlic powder

Spray pan with nonstick spray. Slice or cube sausage. Add to oil and saute with onion for 5 minutes. Pour into slow cooker with remaining ingredients. Cover and cook on low 8 to 10 hours. Serve with hot corn bread or cheese and crackers. Serves 8 to 10.

Per serving: 215 calories; 12.0 fat grams

Foot Note This soup is a crowd pleaser after a cold day of skiing, fishing, football or even work.

ITALIAN SOUP

1 1/2 pounds boneless lean beef stew meat
    (round steak or a roast can be used)
8 cups water
1/2 teaspoon sage
1/2 teaspoon oregano
1/2 teaspoon poultry seasoning
1/2 teaspoon parsley flakes
2 bay leaves
3 garlic cloves, minced
1 teaspoon salt
1/3 cup olive oil
3 beef bouillon cubes
1 tablespoon soy sauce
1 can spaghetti sauce with mushrooms
2 medium potatoes, diced
1 cup carrots, diced
1 medium onion, diced
10 stalks celery, diced
1 green pepper, chopped
1 8-ounce can tomato paste
1 cup elbow macaroni

Trim fat from beef pieces. Put beef into slow cooker. Add remaining ingredients except macaroni. Cover and cook on low 8 to 10 hours. Cook and drain macaroni. Stir into soup in slow cooker. Heat to serving temperature. Serve in soup bowls and top with shredded mozzarella cheese. Serves 12.

Per serving: 241 calories; 10.3 fat grams

Notes:

Side Dishes

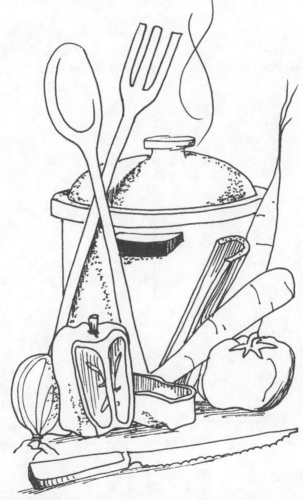

MARINATED FRUIT

This recipe was on the menu when Georgie and Bob helped host a Christmas brunch with friends in Fort Collins. It's one of her favorites for the Holidays.

1 16-ounce can sliced peaches
1 16-ounce can sliced pears
1 13-ounce can pineapple chunks
1 16-ounce can apricots
1 14-ounce jar spiced sliced apple rings
1 14-ounce jar spiced sliced pears
1 11-ounce can mandarin oranges
1/4 cup margarine, melted
1/2 cup sugar
3 tablespoons flour
1 cup drinking sherry
Red food coloring

Drain all fruits well in strainer. Pour into slow cooker. Combine flour and sugar with melted margarine and stir into fruit mixture. Stir in food coloring. Cover and cook on low 4 to 6 hours. Serves 24.

Per serving: 108 calories; 2.1 fat grams

If you prefer smaller pieces of fruit, save time by buying chunk-style peaches and pears in the can.

BAKED APPLES

6 - 8 medium apples, washed and cored
2 tablespoons raisins, optional
1/4 cup brown sugar
1 teaspoon cinnamon
1/4 teaspoon nutmeg
1/4 teaspoon pumpkin pie spice
2 tablespoons butter
1/2 cup water
1 tablespoon lemon juice

Combine raisins, spices and butter together. Place apples in slow cooker; place top layer between apples on bottom layer. Fill cavities with spice mixture. Mix together and pour water and lemon juice over apples. Cover and bake on low 4 to 6 hours. To serve spoon juice from slow cooker over each apple with a scoop of ice cream or frozen whipped cream. Garnish with granola type cereal. Serves 6 to 8.

Per serving: 143 calories; 4.3 fat grams

CHUNKY APPLESAUCE

1/2 cup water
4 cups apples, cored, peeled and cut
    into chunks
1 teaspoon cinnamon
1/2-1 cup sugar

Pour water over apples in slow cooker. Sprinkle with cinnamon and sugar. Cover and cook on low overnight or 8 to 10 hours. If you like it less chunky, use potato masher. Can be served hot or cold. Serves 8.

Per serving: 103 calories; 0.2 fat grams

 For more flavor use apple cider instead of water and add 1/8 teaspoon nutmeg.

LEMON-HONEY PEARS

4 medium pears, pared
Whole cloves
1 cinnamon stick
1/2 cup water
1/2 teaspoon lemon rind, grated
3 tablespoons lemon juice
2 tablespoons honey

Stick 8 whole cloves in each pear. Arrange pears in slow cooker. Combine water, lemon rind, lemon juice and honey together. Pour over pears and drop cinnamon stick in the middle of the four pears. Cover and cook on low 2 to 4 hours. Serve in sherbet dish, spooning sauce from slow cooker over each pear. Garnish with a sprig of mint on each. Serves 4.

Per serving: 300 calories; 11.2 fat grams

PEACH AMBROSIA

4 medium peaches, diced
1/2 cup water
1/2 cup sugar
1 tablespoon butter
Vanilla ice cream
Red or black raspberries

Combine peaches, water, sugar and butter in slow cooker. Cover and cook on low 2 to 4 hours. Remove to serving dish to cool until desired temperature. Scoop ice cream into dessert dish; spoon peaches over ice cream and top with 4 or 5 raspberries. Serves 8.

Per serving: 344 calories; 16.0 fat grams

 Out of this world! Spoon these hot peaches over waffles or pancakes for a special breakfast or brunch.

RHUBARB SAUCE

3 cups rhubarb, diced
1 tablespoon butter
1 cup sugar
1/4-1/2 cup water

Combine ingredients in slow cooker and stir. Cover and cook on low 4 to 5 hours. Can either be served warm or cold.

Per serving: 117 calories; 1.5 fat grams

QUICK idea for dessert: Prepare this the night before and cool. Layer rhubarb, vanilla ice cream and black raspberries in a stemmed wine glass. Start with the rhubarb sauce and end with raspberries. Serve with a fancy cookie and you have a terrific dessert.

ARTICHOKES

4 to 6 artichokes, washed and trimmed
1 - 1 1/2 teaspoon salt
2 cloves garlic, minced
2 cups hot water
2 tablespoons lemon juice (more if more
    lemony taste is desired)
1/2 cup butter, melted
1/2 teaspoon garlic salt
Juice from fresh lemon

Stand artichokes upright in slow cooker; they may be stacked. Add garlic, water and lemon juice. Cook on low 6 to 8 hours. Serve with melted butter, garlic and lemon juice on the side. Serves 4 to 6.

Per serving: 280 calories; 22.9 fat grams

Cyndi uses fresh garlic cloves in almost everything, but in place of it, use garlic salt or seasoned salt.

Add a little parmesan cheese and a hint of white wine to the lemon butter for a change.

BLACK BEANS

1 8-ounce package black beans
1 quart water, or enough to cover beans in
    slow cooker
1 medium onion, chopped
1 garlic clove, minced
1/4 teaspoon salt
1/4 cup fresh cilantro, chopped
1/4 cup salsa
Cheddar cheese, grated

Rinse beans well. Put in slow cooker with onion and garlic. Pour water over all. Cover and cook on low 9 to 10 hours or until beans are soft. Mash beans with potato masher and flavor with salt, cilantro and salsa. Top with cheddar cheese. Serves 8.

Per serving: 164 calories; 5.5 fat grams

 Black beans are great as a side dish or served as a dip with chips spiced up with onion and salsa.

REFRIED BEANS (FRIJOLES)

1 pound dried pinto beans
1 small onion, chopped, optional
1 clove garlic, minced
Enough water to cover beans
1/2 teaspoon salt
1/4 teaspoon dried red-pepper flakes or seasoned pepper
Cheddar cheese, grated, optional

Wash beans very well (beans sometimes have pieces of dirt and/or rocks in them). Put beans, onions and garlic into slow cooker with water to cover the beans by 2 to 3 inches. Cover and cook on low 10 to 11 hours. Partially mash beans with potato masher. Stir in salt and red-pepper flakes. Serve in tortillas as burritos or as a side dish to another Mexican food entree. Top with cheese. Serves 10.

Per serving: 158 calories; 0.5 fat grams

 Add salsa and cheese for a dip for chips.

BEAN CASSEROLE

1/2 cup bacon, cut up
1 15-ounce can lima beans
1 15-ounce can butter beans
1 16-ounce can pork and beans
1 16-ounce can kidney beans
4 large onions, sliced
2 cloves garlic, minced
1 tablespoon brown sugar
1/2 cup vinegar

Brown bacon in skillet. Drain. Mix bacon, beans, onions, garlic, sugar and vinegar in slow cooker. Cook on low 6 to 8 hours. Serves 12.

Per serving: 356 calories; 6.2 fat grams

 These beans are great to take to a potluck or an outdoor barbecue.

SWEDISH RED CABBAGE

1 medium head red cabbage, sliced
2 tart apples, sliced
1/4 cup onion, chopped
2 tablespoons vinegar
1/2 teaspoon caraway seeds
1/2 teaspoon salt
1/4 teaspoon pepper
1/2 cup grape jam or jelly

Place cabbage, apples and onions in slow cooker. Combine remaining ingredients and pour over cabbage mixture. Cover and cook on low 4 to 6 hours. Serve hot with meat course. Serves 10.

Per serving: 77 calories; 0.3 fat grams

SOUTHERN BLACK-EYED PEAS

Georgie and Cyndi both have friends from the south who serve black-eyed peas on New Years Eve to bring good luck for the new year.

1 16-ounce package black-eyed peas
4 slices lean bacon, cut into 1/4-inch pieces
1/2 green pepper, finely chopped
1/2 red pepper, finely chopped
1 small onion, chopped
1/2 cup celery, chopped
1 teaspoon red wine vinegar
1/4 teaspoon ground pepper
1 or 2 hot red peppers, crumbled
2 cups chicken broth or 2 bouillon cubes
    dissolved in 2 cups hot water
3 to 4 cups water

Rinse peas well and drain. Cook bacon until crisp. Drain. Put beans into slow cooker. Add bacon, peppers, onion, celery, vinegar, broth, salt, pepper, hot peppers and water. Cover and cook on low 6 to 8 hours. Serve with hot corn bread. Serves 8.

Per serving: 237 calories; 3.0 fat grams

Foot Note

For QUICK good luck, open a can of black-eyed peas, add all ingredients except broth and water, and serve hot or cold as a dip for crackers.

"BAKED" NEW POTATOES

2 pounds (about 12 to 15) small new pota-
    toes, scrubbed, not peeled
1 10-ounce can cream soup (cheese, mush-
    room, chicken, or celery)
1/4 cup sour cream
2 tablespoons water
2 tablespoons green onion, chopped
2 medium cloves garlic, minced
1 teaspoon dill weed
1/2 teaspoon salt

Place washed potatoes in slow cooker. Stir together remaining ingredients and pour over potatoes. Cover and cook on low 5 to 6 hours. Serves 6.

Per serving: 157 calories; 4.9 fat grams

NO PEEK VEGETABLE CASSEROLE

4 medium carrots, washed and sliced
   on diagonal
4 medium potatoes, washed, peeled and
   sliced on diagonal
3/4 teaspoon salt
2 tablespoons butter or margarine
1 10-ounce cream of mushroom soup
1 soup can water

Place vegetables in slow cooker in layers, ending with carrots. Sprinkle each layer with salt and dot with butter. Mix soup and water together and pour over vegetables. Cover and cook on low 4 to 6 hours. Serves 8.

Per serving: 109 calories; 5.6 fat grams

SWEET POTATOES WITH CRUMB TOPPING

6 sweet potatoes, peeled
1/2 cup water
3/4 cup sugar
1/2 teaspoon salt
3 tablespoons butter or margarine
2 eggs
1/2 cup milk
1 teaspoon vanilla

Topping:

1 cup brown sugar
1/3 cup flour
3 tablespoons butter or margarine
1 cup pecans or walnuts, chopped

Cut sweet potatoes into 2-inch pieces and place in slow cooker. Add water, sugar, salt and butter. Cover and cook on low 6 to 8 hours. Preheat oven to 350°. Remove from slow cooker to a 9"x 9" casserole dish sprayed with nonstick spray. Beat eggs, milk and vanilla together and pour over potatoes. Using fork or pastry blender, cut margarine into sugar and flour. Stir in nuts and spread evenly over potatoes. Bake at 350° for 35 minutes. Serves 6.

Per serving: 511 calories; 20.2 fat grams

Serve with your Thanksgiving turkey dinner or Christmas ham. Cook potatoes overnight, so they will be ready for the next step in the morning.

ALMOND VEGETABLES MANDARIN

1 cup carrots, thinly sliced
1 cup green beans, cut in 1" pieces
1 cup cauliflower, thinly sliced
1/2 cup green onion, sliced
1 6-ounce package frozen pea pods
1 cup water
2 cubes chicken bouillon
1 tablespoon soy sauce
1/4 teaspoon garlic powder
2 teaspoons cornstarch
4 tablespoons water
1/2 cup slivered almonds

Combine carrots, green beans, cauliflower, onion, pea pods, 1 cup water, bouillon, soy sauce and garlic powder in slow cooker. Cover and cook on low 5 to 6 hours. About 15 minutes before serving, mix together cornstarch and water. Stir into vegetable mixture. Cover and cook enough to thicken slightly. Serve topped with almonds. Serves 6.

Per serving: 107 calories; 6.6 fat grams

"BAKED" SQUASH

1 or 2 squash with hard outside shell (acorn or butternut)
1/2 cup water
Salt and pepper
1 teaspoon butter or margarine
1 small onion, sliced

Wash and seed squash; cut in halves, lengths or slices. Place in slow cooker. Add water; sprinkle with salt and pepper. Dot each piece of squash with butter. Lay slices of onion on top of each. Cover and cook on low 5 to 6 hours.

Per serving: 81 calories; 1.1 fat grams

 Baked squash variations.
1. Stuff with other vegetable mixtures.
2. Stuff with meat mixtures.
3. Use a variety of spices, i.e. oregano, thyme, basil, cumin.
4. Add casserole ingredients, i.e. creamed soups, canned or frozen vegetables or fruits.
5. Georgie's favorite: fill buttered acorn squash half with applesauce then sprinkle with cinnamon.

STUFFED ACORN SQUASH

1/2 pound meatloaf mixture, or bulk sausage
1 egg, slightly beaten
12 saltine crackers, crushed
1 teaspoon Dijon mustard
1/4 teaspoon nutmeg
2 tablespoons frozen orange juice concen-
    trate, or 1/4 cup orange juice
2 acorn squash, halved, washed and seeded

In small bowl, mix together sausage, egg, crackers, mustard, nutmeg and orange juice. Fill cavity of squash with meat mixture. Place prepared squash in slow cooker (an oblong style works good for this recipe). Cover and cook on low 5 to 6 hours. When serving, spoon cooking juices from slow cooker over squash. Serves 4.

Per serving: 373 calories; 25.3 fat grams

Variation:

1/4 pound bulk sausage
1 small onion, chopped
1/2 small apple, peeled and chopped
1 cup cabbage shredded
1 tablespoon slivered almonds
Salt and pepper to taste
1/8 teaspoon ground thyme
1/4 teaspoon ground sage

Variation: Mix all ingredients and stuff squash. Cover and cook on low 5 to 6 hours. Serves 4.

Per serving: 152 calories; 12.7 fat grams

 To bring out more of a fruity flavor, use toasted raisin bread, crumbled.

MEXICAN SUMMER SQUASH

1 medium yellow squash, cut into
   1/2-inch slices
1 medium zucchini, cut into 1/2-inch slices
1 medium onion, chopped finely
1 clove garlic, or 1/2 teaspoon garlic salt
1 14-ounce can cream-style corn
1 4-ounce chopped green chiles
1/2 teaspoon ground cumin

Put all ingredients into slow cooker. Stir. Cover and cook on low 5 to 6 hours. Serves 4.

Per serving: 99 calories; 0.7 fat grams

Foot Note If you have time before serving, preheat oven to 350°. Spray a warm 9" x 13" casserole dish with vegetable cooking spray. Pour contents of slow cooker into the casserole dish. Top with generous amount of cheddar cheese and bake in oven 15 to 20 minutes, until cheese is melted and bubbly.

BUTTERNUT SQUASH AND APPLE MEDLEY

1 large or 2 small butternut squash
3 baking apples, cored and cut into
    1/2-inch slices
1/2 cup brown sugar
1/4 cup butter or margarine, melted
1 teaspoon salt
1/4 teaspoon cinnamon
1/4 teaspoon nutmeg

Wash and cut squash in half. Remove seeds and cut into 1/2-inch slices. Put into slow cooker. Place apple slices over squash. Stir together remaining ingredients; sprinkle over apples and squash. Cover and cook on low 6 hours. Serves 6.

Per serving: 194 calories; 7.9 fat grams

ZUCCHINI "CASSEROLE"

1 medium zucchini, sliced
1/3 cup green pepper, chopped
1/2 cup onion, chopped
1 clove garlic, minced
1/2 teaspoon dry Italian salad dressing seasoning
1/2 teaspoon salt
1/4 teaspoon pepper
1 16-ounce can tomatoes, cut up
Mozzarella cheese
Parmesan cheese

Cut zucchini, green pepper, onion and garlic into slow cooker. Sprinkle with seasoning, salt and pepper. Pour tomatoes over all. Cover and cook on low 5 to 6 hours. Serve as a side dish topped with cheeses. Serves 4.

Per serving: 65 calories; 2.8 fat grams

 This goes well with scrambled eggs for breakfast, especially during summer time when the vegetables are fresh.

ITALIAN ZUCCHINI

1 medium zucchini, quartered
1/2 cup onion, chopped
1/2 cup green pepper, chopped
1 6-ounce can tomato paste
1 3-ounce can sliced mushrooms, drained
1 package spaghetti sauce mix
1 cup water
1 cup Mozzarella cheese, shredded

Place zucchini in slow cooker. Mix together onion, green pepper, tomato paste, mushrooms, spaghetti sauce mix and water. Pour over zucchini. Cover and cook on low 6 to 8 hours. To serve, sprinkle with shredded cheese. Serves 4.

Per serving: 171 calories; 7.6 fat grams

 Slice the zucchini and double this recipe to take to a potluck.

CHEESE STUFFED ZUCCHINI

2 medium zucchini
1/4 cup onion, finely chopped
1 tablespoon butter
3/4 cup cream-style cottage cheese
1/2 pound fresh mushrooms, chopped
2/3 cup rice, uncooked
1 egg, slightly beaten
1 tablespoon parsley
1/4 teaspoon salt
1/2 teaspoon dried basil, crushed
2 slices sharp processed American cheese,
    cut in 16 strips

Trim ends of zucchini; cut in half lengthwise. Scoop out center of squash and dice. Dot center of each zucchini with butter. Combine chopped zucchini, onion, cottage cheese, mushrooms, rice, egg, parsley, salt and basil. Spoon mixture into center of squash. Place in slow cooker (rectangular style best for this recipe). Cover and cook on low 6 to 7 hours. Serve topped with strips of cheese. (You can preheat oven to 350° and melt cheese for about 5 minutes, or microwave it.) Serves 4.

Per serving: 434 calories; 24.0 fat grams

MEAT STUFFED ZUCCHINI

2 large zucchini, diameter of 3-inches or more
1 1/2 pounds lean ground beef
1/4 cup celery, finely chopped
1 tablespoon parsley
1 teaspoon salt
1/4 teaspoon pepper
1/2 teaspoon oregano
1 1/4 cups dry bread crumbs, finely crumbled
2 tablespoons onion, grated
1 1/2 teaspoons Worcestershire sauce
1 16-ounce tomatoes, cut in pieces
2 eggs, slightly beaten
1 quart spaghetti sauce
Parmesan cheese

Trim end off zucchini. Hollow out zucchini, leaving about one half-inch shell. Cut into 2 pieces. Place in slow cooker (rectangular cookers work best for this recipe). Use chopped pulp in meat mixture or freeze for use another time. Combine beef, celery, parsley, salt, pepper, oregano, bread crumbs, onion, Worcestershire sauce, tomatoes and eggs in large bowl. Mix well. Stuff zucchini with meat mixture. Pour spaghetti sauce over zucchini. Cover and cook on low 7 to 8 hours. Five minutes before serving, place stuffed zucchini on warm platter. Let stand five minutes before slicing. Slice into 1 to 1 1/2 - inch slices. Serve on warm plates with extra hot spaghetti sauce and top with parmesan cheese. Can be frozen for another meal, so why not double the recipe (stack it in the slow cooker)? Serves 6.

Per serving: 633 calories; 35.6 fat grams

Notes:

Main Dishes

BEER POT ROAST

4-6 pound roast of choice (Cyndi prefers
    rump roasts)
1 stalk celery, chopped
1 16-ounce package baby carrots
1 8-ounce package frozen green beans
4 large potatoes, cleaned, halved
1 onion, sliced
2 garlic cloves
1 teaspoon oregano
1 teaspoon seasoned salt
1/2 teaspoon pepper
2 bay leaves
4 beef bouillon cubes
1 cup water
1 12-ounce can beer
Parsley

Gravy (Optional):

3 cups broth
6 tablespoons butter
6 tablespoons flour
1 cup light sour cream
1/4 cup prepared horseradish

Cut excess fat from roast; rinse in water. Place in slow cooker. Add remaining ingredients in the order given. Cover and cook on low for 6-8 hours. To serve, remove to platter and surround with vegetables. Spoon broth over meat and vegetables. Sprinkle with parsley. Serves 8.

Per serving: 559 calories; 35.8 fat grams

Gravy: Pour all of broth into bowl and set aside. In a medium saucepan, melt butter (you can use oil); stir in flour. Slowly add broth, stirring until smooth and thickened. Stir in sour cream and horseradish.

Per serving: 188 calories; 15.4 fat grams

 The broth from this roast makes a delicious base for soups, casseroles or gravies. Use the leftover roast to make another meal, like BBQ, hot roast beef sandwiches, cold sandwiches or a soup.

MUSHROOM POT ROAST

3 to 4 pound beef roast (chuck, rump, or
    round)
1/4 cup flour
2 tablespoons cooking oil
Salt and pepper
2 onions, sliced
1 1/2 cups water
1/4 cup catsup
1/3 cup cooking sherry
1/2 teaspoon garlic salt
1/4 teaspoon prepared mustard
1/4 teaspoon marjoram
1/4 teaspoon rosemary
1/4 teaspoon thyme
1 bay leaf
1 6-ounce can mushrooms with juice, sliced
    or pieces and stems

Gravy:

Juices from roast plus water to make 4 cups
3 tablespoons flour
1/3 cup cold water

Dredge meat in flour and brown on all sides in oil.
Season with salt and pepper. Place in slow cooker.
Add onion. Mix remaining ingredients and pour
over roast. Cover and cook on low 8 to 10 hours.
To serve, remove roast to warm plate. Slice meat
and offer au jus. Serves 8.

Per serving: 432 calories; 30.2 fat grams

Au jus gravy: Mix flour and water until smooth.
Turn slow cooker to high. Add flour mixture to
juices in slow cooker. Stir occasionally until thickened. More flour and water mixture will make
gravy thicker. Serves 8.

Per serving: 19 calories; 0.2 fat grams

OLD-FASHIONED BOILED DINNER

3 to 4 pound corned beef brisket
3/4 cup water
2 turnips, sliced
8 small onions
8 carrots, cut in desired lengths
5 potatoes, pared and quartered
1 medium cabbage, cored and cut in wedges
Caraway seed, optional

Place brisket in slow cooker. Add remaining ingredients in order given. Cook on low 8 to 10 hours. When ready to serve, remove brisket to warm platter. Slice into thin diagonal pieces. Arrange vegetables around meat slices. Serves 8.

Per serving: 386 calories; 22.7 fat grams

GUESTS FOR DINNER BARBECUED BRISKET

4 to 5 pound beef brisket
1/2-3/4 bottle liquid smoke
1 onion, sliced
1/2 teaspoon celery salt
1/2 teaspoon garlic salt
1/2 teaspoon onion salt
Salt and pepper to taste
4 tablespoons Worcestershire sauce
6 ounces barbecue sauce

Place brisket in slow cooker. Add remaining ingredients, except barbecue sauce. Cover and cook on low 8 hours. One hour before serving, slice brisket and add barbecue sauce. Cover and cook on low 1 hour. Serves 12-15.

Per serving: 392 Calories; 32.4 fat grams

 Foot Notes Can be served on your favorite bun with salad and vegetables.

Can be reheated in slow cooker for 4 to 5 hours. Add a little water or more barbecue sauce to keep the meat moist.

BEEF STROGANOFF

1 pound round steak, cut in 3/4" pieces
1/4 cup flour
1 teaspoon salt
Dash of seasoned salt
Dash of pepper or seasoned pepper
2 1/2 cups onion, chopped
3/4 cup green pepper, diced
1 clove garlic, minced
1 pound fresh mushrooms or 1 4-ounce can
1 10-ounce can condensed consomme or 2
    bouillon cubes, dissolved
1 tablespoon Worcestershire sauce
1 dash hot pepper sauce, optional
1 cup light sour cream
Parsley
Cooked wide noodles

Combine flour and seasonings; roll meat in mixture. Put in slow cooker. Add all other ingredients in order given, except sour cream, parsley and noodles. Cover and cook on low 8 to 10 hours. About 30 minutes before serving, add sour cream and stir all of ingredients. Cover and cook another 30 minutes while noodles are cooking. Serve over noodles and garnish with parsley. Serves 4.

Per serving: 526 calories; 16.4 fat grams

Serve with your favorite coleslaw or fruit salad and rye bread.

BURGUNDY BEEF

2 pounds round steak, cut into 1-inch cubes
2 tablespoons cooking oil
1 1/2 tablespoons flour
1 teaspoon salt
1/4 teaspoon marjoram leaves
1/4 teaspoon thyme leaves
1/8 teaspoon pepper
5 medium onions, sliced
1/2 pound mushrooms, trimmed and sliced, or
    1 8-ounce can sliced mushrooms, drained
3/4 cup beef broth or bouillon
1 1/2 cups red Burgundy wine

Dredge meat in flour. In medium skillet, brown meat in oil and remove to slow cooker. Add other ingredients. Cover and cook on low 8 to 10 hours. Serves 6 to 8.

Per serving: 316 calories; 17.5 fat grams

Serve this wonderful "stew" over cooked, buttered noodles with a large tossed salad and bread. You can serve as a soup, too, with salad and bread.

STEAK DIANE

4 4-ounce beef tenderloin steaks (1-inch thick)
1/2 teaspoon coarsely ground pepper,
1 teaspoon margarine
1/4 cup dry red wine
2 tablespoons lemon juice
1 tablespoon Worcestershire sauce
2 teaspoons Dijon mustard
1 1/2 teaspoons browning and seasoning sauce
1 tablespoon flour
1/4 cup water

Sprinkle pepper over steaks and arrange in slow cooker. Combine wine, lemon juice, Worcestershire sauce, Dijon mustard, and seasoning sauce. Pour over steaks. Cover and cook on low 4 to 6 hours. About 15 minutes before serving, turn slow cooker to high. Remove steaks to warm plates and keep warm. Mix flour and water in small bowl until smooth and add to juices in slow cooker. Stir until thickened. Spoon over steaks. Serves 4.

Per serving: 351 calories; 26.9 fat grams

 Foot Note Your guests will love it!! Serve with baked potatoes, fresh asparagus, salad and bread.

SWEET AND SOUR BEEF

2 pounds round steak, cut in 1-inch cubes
1/4 cup flour
2 tablespoons cooking oil
1 cup water
1/2 cup catsup
1/4 cup brown sugar
1/4 cup vinegar
1 tablespoon Worcestershire sauce
1 teaspoon salt
1 cup onion, chopped
Pimiento
Parsley

Coat steak pieces with flour. In skillet, brown steak and transfer to slow cooker. Combine water, catsup, brown sugar, vinegar, Worcestershire sauce, salt and onion in small mixing bowl. Pour over steak and mix well. Cover and cook on low 6 to 8 hours. Serve over rice, noodles or Chinese noodles. Garnish with pimiento and parsley. Serves 6.

Per serving: 400 calories; 22.9 fat grams

BEEF FAJITAS

1 1/2 pounds flank steak, sliced
1 package fajita seasoning mix
1 large onion, sliced
1 large green pepper, sliced
Refried beans
Salsa
Lettuce
Guacamole
Light sour cream
Tomatoes
Black Olives
Chives
Flour tortillas

Slice flank steak into thin slices. Prepare fajita mix according to package directions. Pour over meat. Add onion and pepper. Cover and cook on low 6 to 8 hours. Serve with any or all of the other ingredients wrapped in a warm flour tortilla. Serves 6 to 8.

Per serving: 380 calories; 17.7 fat grams

STUFFED FLANK STEAK

1 1/2 cups corn bread stuffing mix
1 3-ounce can mushrooms, sliced, with juice
2 tablespoons butter or margarine, melted
1 tablespoon parmesan cheese
1-1 1/2 pounds flank steak, scored both sides
2 tablespoons salad oil
1 3/4-ounce package brown gravy mix
1/4 cup dry red wine
2 tablespoons green onions, minced
1/4 cup current jelly

Combine stuffing with mushrooms and juice, butter and cheese. Spread over flank steak; roll up like jelly roll and fasten with skewers or string. Pour oil in slow cooker. Roll steak in oil, coating all sides. Prepare gravy mix according to directions on package. Mix gravy, wine and onions and pour over meat. Cover and cook on low 8 to 10 hours. Remove meat to platter, slice. Add jelly to sauce in slow cooker and stir until dissolved. Spoon over each serving of meat. Serves 6.

Per serving: 425 calories; 25.0 fat grams

 The stuffing and jelly in combination with the meat and sauce makes a nice gourmet main dish.

STEAK DINNER IN A "POT"

3 medium potatoes, quartered
1 large onion, chopped
1 10-ounce frozen Italian green beans, or
    10-ounce can seasoned French style
    green beans
1 2 ounce jar pimiento, chopped and drained
1 pound boneless round steak, cut into serv-
    ing size pieces
1/4 cup flour
1/4 cup catsup
1 tablespoon Worcestershire sauce
1/4 cup green pepper, chopped, or 2 tea-
    spoons bell pepper flakes
1 teaspoon instant beef bouillon
1 teaspoon salt
1/2 teaspoon dried marjoram leaves
1/4 teaspoon pepper
1/4 cup water

Put potatoes, onion, green beans and pimiento in slow cooker. Dredge meat with flour and arrange over vegetables. Combine catsup, Worcestershire, pepper flakes, bouillon, salt, and marjoram leaves, pepper and water. Pour over all ingredients. Cover and cook on low 8 to 10 hours. Serves 4.

Per serving: 349 calories; 14.1 fat grams

For QUICK, use 16-ounce can whole potatoes, drained, reserving liquid to use in place of water listed in recipe.

BEEF AND VEGETABLE KABOBS

2 pounds high quality beef, cut into cubes
2 green peppers, cut into cubes
2 red peppers, cut into cubes
1 large onion, cut into wedges, separated
1 carton fresh mushrooms, halved
Any other vegetable you would like to add
1 package cherry tomatoes
Wooden skewers
1 10-ounce can condensed beef consomme
1/2 cup dry white wine or apple juice
2 tablespoons soy sauce
2 cloves garlic, minced
1/4 teaspoon onion powder
1 tablespoon plus 1 teaspoon cornstarch
8 whole potatoes, scrubbed

Thread meat and vegetables, except tomatoes, on 8 wooden skewers. Lay in rectangular type slow cooker. Mix consomme, wine, soy sauce, garlic, onion powder and cornstarch together in small bowl. Pour over meat and vegetables. Arrange potatoes carefully around kabobs. Cover and cook on low 6 to 8 hours. About 30 minutes before serving, thread cherry tomatoes and mushrooms on skewer and lay on top of kabobs. Have warm plates ready for everyone to help themselves. Serves 8.

Per serving: 358 calories; 16.8 fat grams

 The meat and vegetables will be well done and have a great flavor.

MAKE-AHEAD HAMBURGER SAUCE SUPREME

4 pounds lean ground beef
2 cups celery, chopped
2 cups onion, chopped
2 tablespoons green pepper, chopped
1 14-ounce can or jar spaghetti sauce
2 cups catsup
2 cups mixed vegetable juice
1 4-ounce can mushrooms, undrained and
    chopped
4 tablespoons brown sugar
2 tablespoons prepared mustard
Salt and pepper to taste
Dash garlic salt

Cook ground beef right in slow cooker. Drain off excess fat. Add remaining ingredients; stir. Cover and cook on low 8 to 10 hours. Serves 32. Makes 8 pints.

Per serving: 381 calories; 24.9 fat grams

 Freeze remainder in pint containers. *Uses:*
1. Heat and spoon onto hamburger buns for sandwiches.

2. Cook wide noodles according to directions on package, drain. Add one pint Hamburger Sauce and place in casserole dish. Bake at 350° for 30 minutes. Top with 1/2 cup grated cheddar cheese and black olive slivers.

3. Add one 14-ounce can chili beans and chili powder to taste. Add tomato juice for thinner chili. Heat. Serve in soup bowl and top with shredded cheddar cheese.

4. Rinse 4 chicken breasts. Place in slow cooker and pour sauce over the chicken breasts. Slice one onion and one green pepper on sauce. To serve, sprinkle with parmesan cheese or grated mozzarella cheese.

MEATLOAF

1 1/2 pounds lean ground beef
1/4 cup milk
1/2 teaspoon salt
20 salt-free, fat-free saltine crackers
1/2 cup onion, chopped
2 tablespoons green pepper, chopped, optional
2 tablespoons red pepper, chopped, optional
2 tablespoons celery, chopped, optional
1 4-ounce can tomato sauce
1/2 cup catsup
Catsup for top
6 green pepper rings
4-6 potatoes, quartered

Mix ground beef, milk, salt, crackers, onion, green pepper, celery, tomato sauce and catsup. Shape into loaf and place in slow cooker. Drizzle with catsup and top with green pepper rings. Place potatoes around meatloaf. Cover and cook on low 6 to 8 hours. Serves 6.

Per serving: 425 calories; 25.2 fat grams

 Foot Notes If you peel potatoes, coat with butter or oil to keep from darkening.

Leftover meatloaf makes great sandwiches. Put it on your favorite bread and spread with spicy mustard, steak sauce and/or mayonnaise.

Beef

BARBECUED MEATBALLS

Sauce: *Prepare first in slow cooker and let simmer while preparing meatballs.*

Nonstick spray
1 cup vinegar
2 tablespoons lemon juice
1/2 cup water
1 cup catsup
1 tablespoon molasses
1 teaspoon sugar
1 teaspoon dry mustard
1 teaspoon garlic salt
1/2 medium onion, chopped

Meatballs:

2 pounds lean ground beef
2 teaspoons seasoning salt
1 teaspoon seasoning pepper
1/2 cup onion, finely chopped
1 cup soft bread crumbs or 3/4 cup fat-free
    saltine crackers, crushed
1/2 cup milk

Sauce: Put all ingredients in slow cooker and stir well. Let simmer on high until meatballs are ready.

Meatballs: Mix all ingredients together and form into 1-inch balls. Place on broiler rack and bake in oven at 400° for 10 to 12 minutes. Put browned meatballs into simmering sauce. Cover and cook on low 4 to 6 hours.

Per serving: 331 calories; 20.0 fat grams

 These make delicious hoagies or can be served as an hors d'oeuvre.

STUFFED GREEN PEPPERS

6 small green peppers, remove tops and seeds
1 pound lean ground beef
1/2 cup rice, uncooked
2/3 cup water
1/2 cup onion, chopped
1/2 teaspoon salt, optional
1 6-ounce can tomato sauce
1 cup catsup
1/2 cup water
About 20 mini carrots, washed

Wash green peppers; pat dry and salt cavity. Combine meat, rice, water, onion, salt and tomato sauce in medium bowl and mix well. Stuff peppers about 3/4 full. Place carrots in bottom of slow cooker. Arrange peppers on top of carrots. Mix catsup and water; pour over peppers. Cover and cook on low 6 to 8 hours. Serve on a bed of rice with tomato sauce from slow cooker. Serves 6.

Per serving: 345 calories; 16.1 fat grams

 Foot Note You can substitute ground ham or ground turkey for the ground beef.

LAYERED HAMBURGER CASSEROLE

6 potatoes, peeled and sliced
2 cups celery, sliced
1 pound lean ground beef
1 medium onion, chopped
1 12-ounce can corn with juice or 1 1/2
    cups frozen corn
1 15-ounce can green beans with juice or 1
    1/2 cups frozen green beans
1 teaspoon salt
1/2 teaspoon pepper

Spray slow cooker with nonstick vegetable spray. Layer ingredients in order given. Cover and cook on low 8 to 10 hours. Serves 6.

Per serving: 176 calories; 9.6 fat grams

To give this "casserole" a little zest, use 1 12-ounce can of mixed vegetable juice and eliminate juices from vegetables.

If using frozen vegetables, add 1 cup water.

CABBAGE ROLLS

1 pound lean ground beef
1 egg
3/4 cup whole wheat breadcrumbs
1/4 cup green onions, chopped
1 clove garlic, minced
1/2 teaspoon sage
2 teaspoons Worcestershire sauce
1 1/2 teaspoons paprika
1/4 teaspoon pepper
1/2 cup light sour cream
8 large cabbage leaves
4 cups cabbage, shredded
1 8-ounce can tomato sauce
1/4 cup water

Combine ground beef, egg, breadcrumbs, onion, garlic, sage, Worcestershire sauce, paprika, pepper and sour cream in large mixing bowl. Fill cabbage leaves equally with ground beef mixture; roll up. Put shredded cabbage in bottom of slow cooker. Stack cabbage rolls on top. Mix tomato sauce and water; pour over rolls. Cover and cook on low 8 to 10 hours. Serves 8.

Per serving: 395 calories; 14.7 fat grams

PRIZE-WINNING CABBAGE ROLL UPS

1 head cabbage, trimmed and cored
Hot water
1 pound lean ground beef
1/2 pound light sausage
1/4 teaspoon salt
1/4 teaspoon pepper
2 medium onions, diced
1 egg
1/2 cup uncooked rice
1 16-ounce can sauerkraut
1 16-ounce can tomatoes

Place cabbage in a large bowl of hot water for 5 to 10 minutes while you are preparing ground beef mixture. Separate leaves using the 12 largest leaves. Mix ground beef and sausage; add salt, pepper, onions, egg and rice. Spoon half of the sauerkraut into slow cooker. Divide meat mixture among the 12 selected cabbage leaves; roll and secure with toothpicks. Arrange rolls on top of sauerkraut. Spoon remaining sauerkraut over rolls and pour tomatoes over all. Cover and cook on low 8 to 10 hours. Serves 12.

Per serving: 196 calories; 12.2 fat grams

BURGER BUNDLES

1 pound lean ground beef
1/3 cup evaporated milk
1 cup herb-seasoned stuffing mix
1 10-ounce can cream of mushroom soup
2 teaspoons Worcestershire sauce
1 tablespoon catsup

Mix ground beef with evaporated milk; divide into 5 balls. Prepare stuffing mix according to package directions. On wax paper, flatten each ball into a 6 -inch circle. Spoon 1/4 cup stuffing in center of each and draw meat over stuffing; seal. Place sealed side down in slow cooker. Combine remaining ingredients and pour over bundles. Cover and cook 6 to 8 hours. Serves 5.

Per serving: 385 calories; 22.8 fat grams

STACKED ENCHILADAS

8 corn tortillas
1 1/2 pounds lean ground beef
1/2 teaspoon salt
1/2 teaspoon ground cumin
1 1/2 cups light sour cream
1/2 cup green onions, chopped, including tops
2 10-ounce cans enchilada sauce
3 cups cheddar cheese, grated

Brown and drain ground beef. Mix salt, cumin, sour cream and onions together . Place one tortilla on bottom of slow cooker. Top with 3 to 4 tablespoons of meat mixture. Spoon on one tablespoon enchilada sauce and sprinkle with cheese. Repeat this process ending with a tortilla. Pour remaining enchilada sauce over stack. Cover and cook on low 4 hours. When ready to serve, top with cheese. Serves 6.

Per serving: 718 calories; 52.8 grams

 For a variety, use 3 cups cooked chicken, cut in bite-sized pieces.

SALSA BURROS

1 1/2 pounds lean ground beef
3/4 pound Italian sausage
1/4 teaspoon garlic salt
1/2 teaspoon ground cumin
1 15-ounce can refried beans
1 7-ounce can green chili salsa
1 cup Monterey Jack cheese, grated
8 flour tortillas
1 7-ounce can green chili salsa
2 cups cheddar cheese, grated
2 large fresh tomatoes, chopped
2 green onions, sliced, including tops
1/2 head lettuce, shredded

Brown beef and sausage; drain. Mix garlic salt, cumin, refried beans, one can green chili salsa, and Jack cheese into meat mixture. Pour into slow cooker. Cover and cook on low 4 hours. Fill tortillas with meat mixture; roll and place on warm plate. Top each burro with equal amounts of green chili salsa and cheddar cheese. Microwave to warm salsa and melt cheese. Serve with tomatoes, onions and lettuce. Serves 8.

Per serving: 685 calories; 45.0 fat grams

If time allows, burros can be arranged in a casserole dish and baked at 350° for 15 minutes.

ITALIAN MEAT SAUCE

1 1/2 pounds lean ground beef
3/4 pound Italian sausage
1 medium onion, chopped
2 cloves garlic, chopped
1 small zucchini, sliced, optional
1 4-ounce can mushrooms, optional
1 12-ounce can tomatoes, finely chopped
2 12-ounce cans tomato sauce
1 8-ounce can tomato paste
1 cup water
1 teaspoon salt
3 teaspoons ground oregano
1/2 teaspoon ground thyme
1/2 teaspoon sage
1/2 teaspoon rosemary, crushed
2 bay leaves

Brown ground beef and sausage; drain. Put all ingredients in slow cooker. Stir. Cover and cook on low 6 to 8 hours. Serves 12.

Per serving: 292 calories; 21.0 fat grams

Cyndi uses this meat sauce for pasta dishes, meatball sandwiches and on top of other meats and vegetables. Freeze leftover sauce to use for other QUICK meals.

CHICKEN ALMONDINE

4 chicken breasts, washed and fat removed
1 10-ounce can cream of chicken soup
1 tablespoon lemon juice
1/2 cup mayonnaise
1 cup celery, chopped
1 tablespoon onion, grated
1/2 cup pimientos, sliced
1/2 cup almonds
Potato chips, crushed

Lay prepared chicken breasts in the bottom of the slow cooker. Mix all other ingredients in mixing bowl, except almonds and potato chips. Pour over chicken breasts.. Cover and cook on low 8 to 10 hours. Remove each serving to dinner plate, Spoon extra "gravy" over chicken breast and top with almonds and potato chips. Serves 4.

Per serving: 605 calories; 35.3 fat grams

 Fresh asparagus and tomatoes are especially good with chicken almondine.

CHICKEN BREASTS ALA ROYALE

4-6 chicken breasts, fat and skin removed
1 1/4 cups light sour cream
5 tablespoons lemon juice
3 teaspoons Worcestershire sauce
3 teaspoons celery salt
3 cloves garlic, finely chopped
1 teaspoon salt
1/2 teaspoon white pepper (if you don't
    have this, use black pepper)
1 cup dried bread crumbs
Paprika

Wash and prepare chicken breasts. Lay out on paper towel. Mix sour cream, lemon juice, Worcestershire sauce, celery salt, garlic, salt and pepper in large bowl. Add chicken, coating each piece well; cover and refrigerate overnight. Next morning, put all in slow cooker, cover and cook on low 8 to 10 hours. To serve, spoon sour cream mixture over each piece and top with bread crumbs. Sprinkle with paprika. Serves 4.

Per serving: 521 calories; 7.7 fat grams

Foot Note Dried bread crumbs aren't usually a staple in most cupboards, so make your own: Microwave 3 slices of bread on high for about 2 minutes. Bread will dry out and get brown in places. Make crumbs by whirling in blender or food processor.

HERBED CHICKEN

3 large chicken breasts, skinned, cut in half
Salt and pepper to taste
1 5-ounce can water chestnuts, sliced and drained
1 3-ounce can mushrooms, sliced and drained
2 tablespoons green pepper, chopped
1/4 teaspoon ground thyme
1 10-ounce can cream of chicken or
    mushroom soup
1/2 cup cooking wine
    (Cyndi uses a white or blush wine)

Place chicken breasts in slow cooker. Sprinkle with salt, pepper and thyme. Add water chestnuts, mushrooms and green pepper. Mix together soup and wine; pour over other ingredients. Cover and cook on low 8 to 10 hours. Serves 4.

Per serving: 177 calories; 3.0 fat grams

CREAMY CHICKEN BREASTS

4 to 6 chicken breasts, skinned and halved
1 teaspoon lemon juice
3/4 teaspoon celery salt
Pepper to taste
Paprika to taste
1 10-ounce can cream of mushroom soup
1 10-ounce can cream of celery soup
1/3 cup dry sherry or white wine, optional
Parmesan cheese

Rinse chicken and pat dry with paper towel. Season with lemon juice, pepper, celery salt and paprika. Place in slow cooker. Mix the soups and wine together in mixing bowl and pour over chicken. Sprinkle with parmesan cheese. Cover and cook on low 6 to 8 hours. Serve with rice and your favorite vegetable. Serves 4 to 6.

Per serving: 176 calories; 3.9 fat grams

CHICKEN FAJITAS

2 pounds chicken fajita meat
1 package fajita seasoning mix
1 large onion, sliced
2 green peppers, sliced
Refried beans
Light sour cream
Guacamole
Salsa
Lettuce
Cheddar cheese, grated
Black olives
Flour tortillas

Rinse fajita chicken meat and place in slow cooker. Prepare fajita mix according to directions on package. Pour over chicken. Add onion and green pepper. Cover and cook on low 4 to 6 hours. Serve with any or all of the other ingredients wrapped in a warm flour tortilla. Serves 6 to 8.

Per serving: 338 calories; 13.4 fat grams

CHICKEN CURRY

3 to 4 boneless chicken breasts, cut in cubes
1 small onion, chopped
1 clove garlic, minced
3 tart apples, pared, chopped
1/2 teaspoon curry powder
1/2 teaspoon salt
1/2 cup water
2 to 3 tablespoons flour
1/2 teaspoon curry powder
1 1/2 cups milk

Wash and prepare chicken. Place in slow cooker. Add onion, garlic, apple, 1/2 teaspoon curry powder, salt and water. Cover and cook on low 5 to 6 hours. About 15 minutes before serving, turn slow cooker to high. Mix flour, last 1/2 teaspoon curry powder and milk together. Stir into chicken mixture; heat until thickened and bubbly. Serve over rice. Serves 5 to 6.

Per serving: 255 calories; 4.2 fat grams

ORIENTAL CHICKEN ROLLS

2 to 3 boneless chicken breasts, pounded,
    each cut in two
1 8-ounce can water chestnuts, drained, sliced
1 4-ounce can mushrooms, sliced
1/4 cup green onions, chopped
3/4 cup bottled Russian or French salad dressing
1 tablespoon soy sauce
1 tablespoon sesame seeds

Wash and flatten chicken breasts by pounding between two sheets of waxed paper, or by placing chicken breast in a plastic bag. Mix dressing, soy sauce and sesame seeds in small bowl. Combine water chestnuts, mushrooms, onions and half of the dressing mix in small bowl. Spread equally among chicken breasts. Roll up and secure with toothpick. Place in slow cooker. Top with remaining dressing mix. Cover and cook on low 5 to 6 hours. Serve with hot cooked rice. Serves 4 to 6.

Per serving: 322 calories; 17.9 fat grams

 Foot Note If you would like the chicken browned a bit, remove from slow cooker to pan and place under broiler for about 5 minutes.

CHICKEN CHOW MEIN WITH PEA PODS

3 boneless chicken breasts, cut in bite-
    size pieces
1 green pepper, cut into strips
3 green onions, chopped
1 clove garlic, minced
1 16-ounce can chow mein vegetables, drained
1 cup chicken broth
2 tablespoons soy sauce
Salt and pepper to taste
1 tablespoon cornstarch
1/4 cup water
1 6-ounce package frozen pea pods,
    thawed, and patted dry

Mix chicken, green pepper, onions, garlic, chow mein, vegetables, broth, soy sauce, salt and pepper in slow cooker. Cover and cook on low 5 to 6 hours. About 10 minutes before serving, turn slow cooker to high. Mix cornstarch and water together and stir into chicken. Heat, stirring occasionally, until thickened. Add pea pods and stir just to heat through. Serve over chow mein noodles or hot rice. Serves 4 to 6.

Per serving: 230 calories; 2.4 fat grams

To make your own broth, dissolve 1 bouillon cube in 1 cup of hot water. Cyndi and Georgie freeze chicken broth from other recipes to use when needed

CHICKEN-ARTICHOKE CASSEROLE

4 to 6 boneless chicken breasts, cut into
    bite-size pieces
1 16-ounce can artichoke hearts, not mari-
    nated, drained
2 10-ounce packages frozen broccoli,
    chopped, thawed
1 cup celery, sliced
1 3-ounce jar pimiento, chopped
1 10-ounce can cream of mushroom soup
1/2 cup white wine
1/2 cup light sour cream
1/2 cup cheddar cheese
Hand full of cashews

Lay chicken in bottom of slow cooker. Add artichoke hearts, broccoli, celery, and pimiento. Stir soup, wine and sour cream together and pour over vegetables. Cover and cook on low 5 to 6 hours. Stir; spoon casserole onto warm plates and top with cheese and cashews. Serves 4 to 6.

Per serving: 426 calories; 10.8 fat grams

ORANGE BURGUNDY CHICKEN

2 1/2 to 3 pounds frying chicken, cut up
1/2 cup orange marmalade
1/2 cup orange juice
1/2 cup dry red wine
2 tablespoons cornstarch
2 tablespoons brown sugar, packed
1 tablespoon lemon juice
1 teaspoon salt

Remove skin from chicken Rinse and place in slow cooker. Combine rest of ingredients in a bowl and pour over chicken. Cover and cook on low 6 to 8 hours. Serve with rice and spinach salad. Serves 6.

Per serving: 400 calories; 12.0 fat grams

 To save time, buy chicken already cut up at the store.

SALSA CHICKEN PIE

3 to 4 boneless chicken breasts, cut in bite-
    size pieces
1/2 cup celery, sliced
1 medium onion, coarsely chopped
1 8-ounce can whole kernel corn
1 4-ounce can green chile peppers, diced
1/2 cup salsa
1/2 cup chicken broth
4 teaspoons cornstarch
1/4 cup water
1 8 1/2-ounce corn bread mix
1 1/2 cups cheddar cheese, shredded
1 4-ounce can green chile peppers, diced

Combine chicken, celery, onion, corn, first can of green chile peppers, salsa and chicken broth in slow cooker. Cover and cook on low 6 to 8 hours. Preheat oven to 425°. About 35 minutes before serving, mix cornstarch and water together and stir into chicken mixture. Prepare corn bread mix according to directions on package. Pour chicken mixture from slow cooker to 10" x 6" x 2" sprayed casserole dish. Pour corn bread mix over chicken mixture. Top with cheese and second can of green chiles. Bake in oven at 425° for 25 minutes. Serves 4 to 6.

Per serving: 497 calories; 17.4 fat grams

Although this recipe calls for extra cooking time, it is well worth the wait.

For a crusty top, mix cheese and second can of chiles into corn bread batter before spreading over chicken mixture.

SEASONED TURKEY ROAST

4 pound turkey roast
1 cup apple juice or white wine
1 chicken bouillon cube
1/8 teaspoon seasoned pepper
1/8 teaspoon sage
1/8 teaspoon thyme
1/8 teaspoon oregano
1 bay leaf

Place turkey in slow cooker. Mix apple juice or wine, bouillon cube, pepper, sage, thyme and oregano together; pour over turkey. Cover and cook on low 8 to 10 hours. Serve with your favorite trimmings. Serves 6.

Per serving: 386 calories; 6.8 fat grams

Foot Notes

Use this delicious broth to make gravy. Skim any fat from broth. In small sauce pan, combine 1 cup of broth heated to boiling. Mix together 1/4 cup water and 2 tablespoons flour; add to boiling broth, stirring until thickened. You may add a little more water to make a thinner gravy.

CRANBERRY GLAZED ROAST TURKEY

1 4-pound turkey roast
1 16-ounce can whole or jellied
    cranberry sauce
1/4 cup butter or margarine
1 teaspoon Worcestershire sauce
1/4 cup orange juice
2 teaspoons orange rind, grated
1/8 teaspoon poultry seasoning
2 teaspoons brown sugar

Place turkey roast in slow cooker. Mix together cranberry sauce, butter, Worcestershire sauce, orange juice, orange rind, poultry seasoning and brown sugar. Pour over turkey. Cover and cook on low 8 to 10 hours. Baste turkey with cranberry glaze before removing turkey to warm platter to slice. Offer cranberry sauce on the side for those who want extra. Serves 6.

Per serving: 553 calories; 14.4 fat grams

Instead of turkey, try this recipe with Cornish game hens for a special dinner. A rectangular slow cooker works best for this recipe.

TURKEY POT PIE

2 cups cooked turkey, cut in bite-size pieces
3 medium carrots, cut in 1-inch pieces
1 15-ounce can cut green beans
1 15-ounce can sliced potatoes
1 medium onion, chopped
1 4-ounce can mushrooms, sliced
1/4 teaspoon ground thyme
1/4 teaspoon oregano
1/4 teaspoon salt
1/4 teaspoon pepper
3 tablespoons cornstarch
1 16-ounce can turkey or chicken broth
1 single recipe for pie crust

Put all ingredients except cornstarch, broth and pie crust in slow cooker. Mix cornstarch and broth together until smooth. Stir into ingredients in slow cooker. Cover and cook on low 6 to 8 hours. About 20 minutes before serving, preheat oven to 425°. Pour mixture into a casserole dish that has been sprayed with no stick spray. Lay pie crust on top of that; poke with fork several times. Place in oven and bake 15 minutes until crust is golden brown. Serves 6.

Per serving: 306 calories; 13.8 fat grams

This is a good recipe to use up left-over Thanksgiving turkey.

Prepare the pot pie QUICKly by using an a ready prepared pie crust.

SAUSAGE BEAN COMBO FOR COMPANY

1 pound pork link sausages
1/2 pound smoked ham, cut into 1/2-inch
    cubes
1/2 cup onion, chopped
1 10-ounce package frozen lima beans
3 19-ounce cans baked beans
3 15-ounce cans kidney beans
1 8-ounce can tomato sauce
1/2 cup catsup
1/4 cup brown sugar, packed
1 teaspoon salt
1/2 teaspoon pepper
1/2 teaspoon dry mustard

QUICKly brown sausages in skillet. Drain fat and pat with paper towel. Place in slow cooker. Add all other ingredients. Stir. Cover and cook on low 8 to 10 hours. Serves 10 to 12.

Per serving: 317 calories; 3.8 fat grams

Use Italian link sausages instead of pork links for a different taste.

SAUSAGE STUFFED PUMPKIN

1 small pumpkin, seeded, scraped and cut
    into 6 pieces
2 pounds light sausage
1 pound lean ground beef
1/2 cup celery, chopped
1 medium onion, chopped
4 cups seasoned croutons
1 cup walnuts, chopped
1 cup brown sugar
2 tablespoons orange juice
1/8 teaspoon ginger

Prepare pumpkin and arrange pulp side up in slow cooker. Mix all other ingredients together in large bowl. Spoon on top of pumpkin. Cover and cook on low 8 to 10 hours. Serve each piece of pumpkin with portion of meat mixture. Serves 6.

Per serving: 1046 calories; 80.8 fat grams

 This is fun if you can find a pumpkin that fits right into your slow cooker. Clean it and leave it whole. Put the meat mixture inside. Cover and cook on low 8 to 10 hours. Serve whole on a warm platter. Slice off pumpkin at the table and spoon meat mixture out of pumpkin, serving all on a warm plate.

APPLESAUCE PORK CHOPS

4 lean loin pork chops, trimmed of fat
2 cloves garlic, minced
1/2 teaspoon ground cumin
1/2 teaspoon oregano
1/4 teaspoon nutmeg
1/4 teaspoon red pepper
1/4 teaspoon black pepper
1 1/2 cup applesauce
1 1/2 cup red cabbage
4 potatoes, washed, whole

Place pork chops in slow cooker. Mix garlic, cumin, oregano, nutmeg and peppers in small bowl. Sprinkle over chops. Spread applesauce over chops and top with cabbage. Arrange potatoes around chops. Cover and cook on low 8 to 10 hours. Serves 4.

Per serving: 381 calories; 15.2 fat grams

EASY CHOW MEIN

1 pound lean pork steak, already cut up
1/2 cup onion, chopped
1/2 cup green onion, sliced
1 cup celery, sliced
1/2 teaspoon garlic powder
1 3-ounce can mushrooms, drained, sliced
1 16-ounce can Chinese vegetables, drained
2 cups beef broth
3 tablespoons soy sauce
2 tablespoons browning sauce
3 cups chow mein noodles

Trim fat from pork steak. Cut meat into very thin strips. Place in slow cooker. Add all other ingredients except chow mein noodles. Cover and cook on low 6 to 8 hours. About 15 minutes before serving, turn slow cooker to high. Combine cornstarch and water and stir into chow mein. Continue heating until bubbly and thickened. Serve over rice and top with generous serving of chow mein noodles. Serves 4.

Per serving: 485 calories; 27.5 fat grams

 Use 2 beef bouillon cubes dissolved in 2 cups boiling water in place of beef broth.

CHRISTMAS HAM

1 5-6 pound fully cooked bone-in whole ham
1 teaspoon dried rosemary leaves
3/4 teaspoon ground cloves
1/2 teaspoon ground ginger
1 teaspoon parsley
1 medium onion, peeled and sliced
1 stalk celery with leaves, sliced
1 cup apple cider

Mix rosemary, cloves and ginger together. Trim fat from ham and rub surface with clove mixture. Place ham in slow cooker. Add parsley, onion, celery and apple cider. Cover and cook on low 8 to 10 hours. Place on serving platter. Serve hot or cold. Serves 15 to 20.

Per serving: 143 calories; 8.0 fat grams

 If you want, brown ham in preheated 400° oven 15 minutes. Let cool slightly before slicing.

Ham

SCALLOPED POTATOES AND HAM

This is one of Cyndi's favorite recipes for a cold winter day, served with coleslaw and fresh tomatoes.

8 slices of ham
10 potatoes, peeled and sliced
1 large onion, peeled and sliced
1 stalk celery, sliced, optional
Salt and pepper to taste
1 pound processed American cheese, cut
    in chunks
1 10-ounce can cream of celery or
    mushroom soup

Place ham in slow cooker. Add potatoes, onion, celery. Sprinkle with salt and pepper. Add cheese chunks. Pour soup over all. Cover and cook on low 8 to 10 hours. When ready to serve, mix slightly. Serves 6 to 8.

Per serving: 566 calories; 33.4 fat grams

CRANBERRY HAM

3 to 4 pounds precooked ham, sliced
1 1/2 cups fresh cranberries
3/4 cup honey
1/2 cup hot water
1 30-ounce can sweet potatoes
6 tablespoons brown sugar

Lay ham slices in slow cooker. Cover with cranberries and honey. Arrange potatoes on top and sprinkle with brown sugar. Carefully add water. Cover and cook on low 6 to 8 hour. Serves 6.

Per serving: 694 calories; 24.3 fat grams

 Save time and buy your ham presliced. This is also a great way to use up your leftover hams.

Notes:

Quick, Quick, Quick

QUICK BEEF STEW

1 pound lean stew meat
1 packet stew seasoning mix
1 16-ounce package stew vegetables, sliced
1 15-ounce can tomatoes, chopped
5 cups water

Combine all ingredients in slow cooker. Cook on low 8 to 10 hours. Serves 6.

Per serving: 323 calories; 16.4 fat grams

 According to Georgie, the secret to a good stew is the turnips. You will find them included in the stew vegetables along with potatoes, carrots, onion and celery. Look for these in the produce section of your grocery store.

ROAST BEEF

The following are options for QUICK preparations of roasts. Choose your favorite cut and add vegetables and flavorings. Vegetables can be placed under roast to keep them from browning around the edges.

1 3-pound roast, cut of your choice

Option 1: Salt and pepper

Option 2: 1 package of dry onion soup mix

Option 3: Use a pot roast for this recipe
    1 tablespoon onion flakes
    2 tablespoons Worcestershire sauce
    1 bay leaf
    2 peppercorns
    2 cloves garlic
    1 cup water

4 to 6 potatoes, halved
2 cups baby carrots
4 stalks celery, cut in 3-inch lengths
1 onion, quartered

Place potatoes, carrots, celery and onion in slow cooker. Trim fat from roast. Lay roast on top of vegetables. Top with one of the options given. Cover and cook on low 10 to 12 hours. Serves 6.

Option 1: Per serving: 555 calories; 35.9 fat grams

Option 2: Per serving: 575 calories; 36.3 fat grams

Option 3: Per serving: 575 calories; 36.5 fat grams

 If you have a rack for your slow cooker, you can place the roast on the rack and surround it with the vegetables.

Quick, Quick, Quick

SWISS STEAK

2 pounds round steak, cut in serving sizes
Salt and pepper to taste
1 large onion, thinly sliced
1 16-ounce can stewed tomatoes
Dash of browning sauce

Season steak with salt and pepper and place in slow cooker. Add onion. Pour tomatoes over all ingredients. Cover and cook on high 1 hour; turn to low 6 to 8 hours. Serves 6 to 8.

Per serving: 235 calories; 13.8 fat grams

 Cyndi always adds slices of green pepper. Serve with mashed potatoes and a favorite vegetable or salad.

STEAK AND RICE CASSEROLE

1 pound round steak, cut in cubes
1 10-ounce can mushroom soup
1 can water
1/2 cup rice, uncooked
1 package onion soup mix

Combine ingredients in slow cooker. Cover and
cook on low 6 to 8 hours. Serves 4.

Per serving: 354 calories; 15.6 fat grams

 Add a little variety to this recipe with
some chopped celery and a sprinkling
of basil. Finish off the meal with
your favorite vegetable and salad.

Quick, Quick, Quick

STEAK AND POTATO CASSEROLE

1 1/2 pounds round steak
Flour
Salt and pepper
4 medium potatoes, sliced
1 medium onion, sliced
1/2 cup water

Trim steak and cut into serving pieces. Coat with flour and sprinkle with salt and pepper. Alternate layers of steak, potatoes and onion in slow cooker. Pour water over all ingredients. Cover and cook on low 8 to 10 hours. Serves 4.

Per serving: 412 calories; 20.7 fat grams

To vary this recipe, top with 1 can green beans and 1 can tomato soup, or just add the soup and omit the water. Cover and cook on low 8 to 10 hours.

SLOPPY JOES

3 pounds lean ground beef
2 onions, finely chopped
2 cups catsup
1/2 cup water
1/2 teaspoon garlic salt
1/2 teaspoon pepper
1 tablespoon dry mustard

Brown ground beef in large pan. Drain well (rinsing with water will reduce fat). Pour into slow cooker. Add all remaining ingredients. Mix well. Cover and cook on low 6 to 8 hours. Serve on hamburger buns with dill pickles, cottage cheese, favorite vegetable or potato chips. Serves 12.

Per serving: 348 calories; 23.7 fat grams

Foot Notes

Two packages of Sloppy Joe mix can be used in place of onions, garlic salt, pepper and mustard. Use only 1 cup catsup. Add a little green pepper for added flavor.

Double the recipe. Sloppy Joes freeze well.

HAMBURGER BEANS

1 pound lean ground beef
1/2 pound bacon
1/2 cup onion, chopped
1/2 cup catsup
1/3 cup brown sugar
1 teaspoon dry mustard
2 teaspoons white vinegar
1 teaspoon salt
2 cans pork and beans
1 can barbecue beans

Brown ground beef and bacon; drain. Put into slow cooker. Cover and cook on low 6 to 8 hours. Serves 16.

Per serving: 228 calories; 13.6 fat grams

 This recipe is QUICK and a crowd pleaser at potlucks or picnics.

CORNED BEEF AND CABBAGE

2 pounds corned beef brisket
1 head cabbage
Salt and pepper

Salt and pepper brisket; brown in skillet sprayed with nonstick spray. Put brisket in slow cooker. Quarter the cabbage and place on top of brisket. Cover and cook on low 8 to 10 hours. Serve with bread and sliced tomatoes. Serves 6.

Per serving: 326 calories; 22.5 fat grams

SUPPER IN A POT

4 lean pork chops
1 10-ounce can tomato soup
1/2 cup water
1 teaspoon Worcestershire sauce
1/2 teaspoon salt
1/2 teaspoon oregano
4 medium potatoes, quartered, or 6 to 8
    small whole potatoes
4 carrots, split, or 2 cups baby carrots

Trim fat from pork chops. QUICKly brown chops in skillet. Place in slow cooker. Place potatoes and carrots around chops. Mix soup, water, Worcestershire sauce, salt and oregano together and pour over all ingredients. Cover and cook on low 6 to 8 hours. Serves 4.

Per serving: 370 calories; 15.9 fat grams

EASY PORK DELIGHT

6 pork chops or steaks
1 10-ounce can cream of mushroom soup

Trim fat from chops or steaks. Place in slow cooker. Add soup. Cover and cook on low 6 to 8 hours. Serves 4 to 6.

Per serving: 310 calories; 20.5 fat grams

 Cyndi's Mom likes to add sliced green peppers and onions before pouring soup over chops.

QUICK CHICKEN BREASTS

4 to 6 chicken breasts
1 10-ounce can cream of mushroom soup

Rinse and trim fat from chicken breasts. Place chicken in slow cooker. Pour choice of soup over chicken breasts. Cover and cook on low 5 to 6 hours. Serves 4 to 6.

Per serving: 325 calories; 8.6 fat grams

 Chicken breasts can be slow cooked with a variety of soups-choose the one you like best.

CHICKEN AND COLA

1 fryer, cut into pieces
1 teaspoon salt
1/2 cup catsup
1 12-ounce can cola

Rinse chicken and remove skin, if desired. Place in slow cooker. Mix salt, catsup and cola together and pour over chicken. Cover and cook on low 6 to 8 hours. Serves 6.

Per serving: 332 calories; 12.0 fat grams

Buy the chicken already cut up to save time.

Try chicken wings with this recipe as an appetizer. It's a perfect alternative to your favorite hot wings recipe.

FRUITY BARBECUE CHICKEN

1 chicken, cut up, or your favorite pieces
1 8-ounce bottle Russian dressing
1 packet onion soup mix
1 10-ounce jar apricot preserves

Rinse and remove skin from chicken pieces. Place chicken in slow cooker. Mix dressing, soup mix and preserves and pour over chicken. Cover and cook on low 8 to 10 hours. Serve with potatoes or rice and a green salad. Serves 6.

Per serving: 608 calories; 31.7 fat grams

For a different flavor, remove chicken pieces to a seasoned charcoal grill, and grill for a short time.

BASIL CHICKEN

4 chicken breasts, skinned
1/2 - 3/4 teaspoon pepper or seasoned pepper
1/2 - 3/4 teaspoon basil
1 10-ounce can cream of celery soup
1/2 green pepper, sliced

Place chicken breasts in slow cooker. Sprinkle with pepper and basil. Spread soup on top of chicken. Arrange slices of green pepper on top of soup. Cover and cook on low 6 to 8 hours. Serves 4.

Per serving: 272 calories; 4.2 fat grams

 Always trim fat and rinse chicken before cooking.

HONEY MUSTARD CHICKEN

2 1/2 pounds chicken, your favorite pieces
1/4 cup honey
2 teaspoons lemon juice
1/2 cup Dijon mustard
1/2 teaspoon curry powder

Remove skin from chicken pieces, rinse and place in slow cooker. Mix honey, lemon juice, mustard and curry powder together in a small bowl. Brush over chicken pieces. Cover and cook on low 8 to 10 hours. Serve with fresh or baked tomatoes and brown rice. Serves 6.

Per serving: 299 calories; 10.9 fat grams

FESTIVE PORK CHOPS

6 pork chops, 3/4-inch thick
1/4 teaspoon salt
1/4 teaspoon pepper
1/8 teaspoon ground ginger
2 teaspoons lemon juice
1/2 teaspoon chicken bouillon granules
1 cup cherry pie filling
Parsley

Trim fat from chops and place in slow cooker. Mix remaining ingredients in small bowl. Pour over pork chops. Cover and cook on low 8 to 10 hours. Serve with your favorite salad and rice. Serves 6.

Per serving: 290 calories; 14.8 fat grams

BRATS WITH APPLE-KRAUT

6 bratwurst links, halved crosswise
4 tart apples, peeled, cored and sliced
1 27-ounce can sauerkraut, drained
1/3 cup brown sugar, packed
1 teaspoon caraway seed
1/8 teaspoon nutmeg
1/2 cup water

Stir together all ingredients in slow cooker. Cover and cook on low 6 to 8 hours. Serves 6.

Per serving: 332 calories; 20.0 fat grams

SPARERIBS AND SAUERKRAUT

1 large can sauerkraut
1 large can tomatoes
2 tablespoons sesame seed
1 large onion, chopped
2 pounds spareribs, cut
Salt and pepper

Combine first four ingredients. Pour into slow cooker. Top with spareribs. Salt and pepper to taste. Cover and cook on low 8 to 10 hours. Serves 5.

Per serving: 363 calories; 28.8 fat grams

SCALLOPED PORK CHOPS

1 16-ounce package scalloped potatoes
2 tablespoons pimiento, chopped
4 pork loin chops, about 3/4-inch thick
Salt
Pepper

Trim fat from chops. Spray skillet with nonstick spray and brown chops QUICKly. In the meantime, pour all contents of potato package into slow cooker. Stir in pimiento and water and/or milk called for in the preparation instructions on the package. Stir. Place pork chops on top of potato mixture. Cover and cook on low 4 to 6 hours. Serves 4.

Per serving: 376 calories; 23.1 fat grams

 Whenever possible buy products already chopped, shredded, sliced, or whatever makes cooking faster for you.

BARBECUED MEATS

Beef, chicken or pork

Brisket, roast, round steak, ribs, pieces or even leftover meat can be used in this recipe.

1 cup bottled barbecue sauce

Place cut of choice in slow cooker. Pour prepared barbecue sauce over meat. Cover and cook on low 8 to 10 hours.

Beef per serving: 460 calories; 31.8 fat grams
Chicken per serving: 266 calories; 6.9 fat grams
Pork per serving: 371 calories; 21.1 fat grams

Sliced onions and green peppers can be added for extra flavor.

Combine a variety of leftover beef, chicken or pork to make a meat "bouillabaisse".

Quick, Quick, Quick

EXTRA QUICK MEATBALLS

20 precooked or frozen meatballs
1 cup barbecue sauce

Place meatballs in slow cooker and pour barbecue sauce over them. Cover and cook on low 6 to 8 hours. Serves 4.

Per serving: 320 calories; 14.2 fat grams

Option:

20 precooked or frozen meatballs
1 10-ounce can mushroom soup
2 teaspoons Worcestershire sauce
1 tablespoon catsup

Option: Place meatballs in slow cooker. Mix soup, Worcestershire sauce and catsup together in bowl and pour over meatballs. Cover and cook on low 6 to 8 hours. Serves 4.

Per serving: 357 calories; 19.0 fat grams

 Use for either appetizer or main dish meat accompanied by vegetables and salad. These make great meatball sandwiches topped with your choice of lettuce, sprouts, onions, pickles, olives and cheese.

QUICK ONION ROAST

Flour
3 pound roast
1 packet onion soup mix

Coat roast with flour and place on rack in slow cooker. Sprinkle with soup mix. Cover and cook on low 8 to 10 hours. Serves 6.

Per serving: 501 calories; 35.8 fat grams

 Vegetables can be added to your roasts before cooking. Carrots, potatoes, onions and celery are the usual choices. Be creative and try something different. Georgie likes new potatoes, baby carrots, onions and zucchini slices.

QUICK TURKEY ROAST

Frozen turkey roast
1 packet chicken gravy mix

Remove wrappings from roast. Rinse and place in slow cooker. Cover and cook on low 8 to 10 hours. Remove roast to warm platter. Turn temperature to high. Add enough water to make 1 1/2 cups liquid. Stir in gravy mix with a wisk. Continue heating until thickened. Serve with mashed potatoes or stuffing. Serves 6.

Per serving: 275 calories; 5.1 fat grams

SEASONED PORK ROAST

Georgie's Aunt Sallie introduced her to this QUICK roast idea.

3 pound seasoned pork roast
4 potatoes, quartered
2 cups baby carrots
1 large onion, quartered
1 cup water

Remove plastic wrap but leave the webbing on the roast. Put vegetables in slow cooker. Place frozen pork roast on top of vegetables. Cover and cook on low 8 to 10 hours. Applesauce is a favorite side dish with pork. Serves 6.

Per serving: 838 calories; 55.5 fat grams

 Roasts can be put in the slow cooker frozen. Increase cooking time by 2 hours.

CHERRY-PINEAPPLE TURKEY ROAST

3 pound frozen boneless turkey roast
1 10-ounce jar cherry preserves
1 8-ounce can crushed pineapple
1 tablespoon lemon juice
Dash cloves

Remove wrappings and fat from turkey roast. Place in slow cooker. Combine juice from pineapple, lemon juice and cloves. Pour over turkey. Cover and cook on low 8 to 10 hours. Just before serving, remove roast to warm platter. Turn slow cooker to high. Mix cherry preserves and pineapple with juices in slow cooker and heat. Slice turkey and spoon cherry sauce over slices. Pass remaining sauce. Serves 8 to 10.

Per serving: 238 calories; 3.1 fat grams

QUICK POT ROAST

Flour
3 pound roast
1 tablespoon minced onion
2 tablespoons Worcestershire sauce
2 peppercorns
2 whole cloves
1 large bay leaf
2 cups water

Coat roast with flour and place in slow cooker. Mix remaining ingredients and pour over roast. Cover and cook on low 8 to 10 hours. Serves 6 to 8.

Per serving: 502 calories; 36.0 fat grams

 For a QUICK gravy, stir 1 package of gravy mix of your choice into juices from roast and enough water to make 1 1/2 cups liquid.

Quick, Quick, Quick

CHERRY GLAZED PORK ROAST

3 pound pork roast
1 10-ounce can chicken broth
8 green onions, halved lengthwise and cut
   in 2-inch pieces
3 tablespoons raspberry or red wine vinegar
1 teaspoon rosemary
1 cup cherry jam

Remove any extra fat from roast. Place in slow cooker. Mix all ingredients except cherry jam in small bowl. Pour over roast. Cover and cook on low 8 to 10 hours. Just before serving, turn slow cooker to high. Remove roast to warm platter. Mix cherry jam with juices in slow cooker and heat to serving temperature. Spoon over sliced pork and garnish with crosswise slices of green onion tips. Serve with spinach salad or favorite green vegetable. Serves 8 to 10.

Per serving: 557 calories; 33.5 fat grams

HELEN'S LEFTOVER ROAST "CASSEROLE"

Georgie has fond memories of this recipe and of her friend's mother, Helen, who fixed it for her. It is excellent! What a way to use leftovers all in one meal.

Leftover roast, cut in cubes
Leftover potatoes, cut in chunks
Leftover carrots, cut in slices
Leftover vegetables
Leftover gravy

Combine all ingredients. "Dump" into slow cooker. Cover and cook on low 4 to 6 hours.

Calories and fat grams vary

Quick, Quick, Quick

BRAD'S QUICK BEEF AND NOODLES

3 pounds stew meat, trimmed
1 large onion, chopped
1 tablespoon paprika
Salt to taste
Pepper to taste
2 10-ounce cans beef broth

Mix all ingredients in slow cooker. Cover and cook on high 4 hours. Turn to low and cook 4 to 6 hours. Serve over noodles. Serves 6.

Per serving: 731 Calories; 48.0 fat grams

 If you prefer thicker juices, mix 1/4 cup water with 1/4 cup cornstarch and stir into meat mixture.

PORK CHOPS ALA QUICK

4 lean pork chops
2 cups baby carrots
3 stalks celery, cut in 3-inch lengths
1 medium green pepper, sliced
1 medium onion, sliced
Salt and pepper
1 10-ounce can cream of mushroom or
    cream of celery soup

Arrange carrots and celery on bottom of slow cooker. Trim pork chops and place on top of carrots. Arrange slices of pepper and onion on top of chops. Salt and pepper to taste. Cover and cook on low 6 to 8 hours. Serves 4.

Per serving: 371 calories; 21.2 fat grams

 Cyndi's Mom uses this recipe for those extra busy days.

Quick, Quick, Quick

Notes:

Index

Index

Notes:

Name _____

Address _____

City/State/Zip _____

Telephone (_____) _____

Please send best-selling cookbooks as indicated below:

	QUANTITY	PRICE	TAX (Colorado Residents Only)	TOTAL
COLORADO COOKIE COLLECTION	_____	$ 14.95	$ .45 per book	$_____
NOTHIN' BUT MUFFINS	_____	$ 12.95	$ .39 per book	$_____
101 WAYS TO MAKE RAMEN NOODLES	_____	$ 9.95	$ .30 per book	$_____
MYSTIC MOUNTAIN MEMORIES	_____	$ 14.95	$ .45 per book	$_____
COOKIE EXCHANGE	_____	$ 12.95	$ .39 per book	$_____
QUICK CROCKERY COOKING	_____	$ 14.95	$ .45 per book	$_____

TOTAL ENCLOSED _____

☐ Check   ☐ Money Order   ☐ Visa   ☐ MasterCard

Please make checks Payable to: Please See Reverse   Please See Reverse

C & G Publishing, Inc.
P.O. Box 5199
Greeley, CO 80632
(800) 925-3172

If using Visa or MasterCard, please fill in the following:

Name _____

Address _____

City/State/Zip _____

Telephone (_____) _____

Please charge this order to my ☐ Visa   ☐ MasterCard

Account Number ⬚⬚⬚⬚⬚⬚⬚⬚⬚⬚⬚⬚⬚⬚⬚⬚⬚⬚

Expiration Date _____ / _____
                month   year

Customer Signature _____